Jeff + Milton,

You both are such wonderful gifts in my life. Thank you for your presence and your friendship —

You love
Michael

Healing Within

My Journey with Breast Cancer

Michael W. Kovarik

BALBOA
PRESS
A DIVISION OF HAY HOUSE

Copyright © 2014 Michael W. Kovarik.

All rights reserved. No part of this book may be used or reproduced by any means, graphic, electronic, or mechanical, including photocopying, recording, taping or by any information storage retrieval system without the written permission of the publisher except in the case of brief quotations embodied in critical articles and reviews.

Cover Design: Mario Bruni, Silver Horse Studios
www.silverhorsestudios.com

Edited by Kaitlyn Tolman/Louise H. Jones

Author photo by Tom Watkins
www.watkinstom.com

Balboa Press books may be ordered through booksellers or by contacting:
Balboa Press
A Division of Hay House
1663 Liberty Drive
Bloomington, IN 47403
www.balboapress.com
1 (877) 407-4847

Because of the dynamic nature of the Internet, any web addresses or links contained in this book may have changed since publication and may no longer be valid. The views expressed in this work are solely those of the author and do not necessarily reflect the views of the publisher, and the publisher hereby disclaims any responsibility for them.

The author of this book does not dispense medical advice or prescribe the use of any technique as a form of treatment for physical, emotional, or medical problems without the advice of a physician, either directly or indirectly. The intent of the author is only to offer information of a general nature to help you in your quest for emotional and spiritual well-being. In the event you use any of the information in this book for yourself, which is your constitutional right, the author and the publisher assume no responsibility for your actions.

Any people depicted in stock imagery provided by Thinkstock are models, and such images are being used for illustrative purposes only.
Certain stock imagery © Thinkstock.

Printed in the United States of America.

ISBN: 978-1-4525-1622-6 (sc)
ISBN: 978-1-4525-1624-0 (hc)
ISBN: 978-1-4525-1623-3 (e)
Library of Congress Control Number: 2014909994

Balboa Press rev. date: 6/9/2014

To Tim: You are my partner in life, my rock, and my best friend.

To my mom, Helen, my sister, Janet, and my brother, Chuck: Thank you for opening your hearts and sharing the love you hold dear.

To Felicitas Anderson: You are my guardian angel here on Earth.

To Ronnie Delancey-Smith: You are family.

In memory of my dad, Charlie: Of course I loved you too.

When listening to our inner voice, we embrace its message, treasure its guidance, and trust its love. This comforting, intimate instrument gently guides us in discovering our authentic self, one's genuine life path, and the potential we possess to truly heal within.

—Michael W. Kovarik

Contents

Introduction xi
The Journey Begins 1
The Gifts Begin 4
Finding Strength 11
Breathe 13
Crossroads 14
Denial, Learning, and Searching 19
Change 22
The Opening of New Paths to Learning 24
Trust 31
Surrender 33
Crossing Paths 42
My Spirit Speaks 48
Making a Change 51
Saying Good-bye 56
Exploring New Realms 59
Delving into Buddhist Peace 71
Psychic Connections 77
As My Heart and Mind Open, More Healers Enter 85
A Time of Reflection 94
Knock, Knock, It's the Universe Calling 97
Tattoo Becoming Whole: Physically and Emotionally 102
Insight to a New Direction 106
Westward Bound 109

The Gifts Unwrapped 110
A New Path Unfolds 115
Awakened 118
In the Present 122
Helpful Connections 127
Acknowledgments 131
Bibliography 135
About the Author... 141

Introduction

...actions and words come forth softly, like the changing...
...rom that state of balance, you'll find clarity and peace.

Dan Millman

...e to be from my journey with cancer—not once, but ...th has been filled with fear, joy, laughter, tears, and ...y when the student is ready, the teacher will come. How true, for I have been fortunate to be in the presence of many wonderful souls who have been my teachers.

My passage to healing evolved over a few years. It did not happen right away, but rather it occurred when I was ready for it to begin. First, I had to be awakened to this path and perfect the balance within. As I reflect back, I am truly amazed by and grateful to this disease. It is this disease, so grounded in dread and fear, that had the power to awaken me to my heart, my soul, and the quest they were guiding me to be part of. Gazing into my past, I see the transformation of an individual so rooted in trepidation into one in whom the light was given permission to finally enter. This light was a pathway that opened inner doors and introduced freedom where my true self emerged.

As a child, I struggled to understand myself. The fear residing within was so powerful, I shut down emotionally and spiritually. Growing up gay and Catholic in an era when the two could never meet fed this terror inside, which in turn hid who I was as a person. I was frightened of anyone knowing the real me, which greatly influenced how I felt about and viewed myself, along with my interactions with others. The belief I held that I was not good enough and could not love myself invaded every aspect of my being. For most of my life, I was a scared, shy, and insecure individual, choosing to deny my own power. This toxic behavior and belief seeped into the essence of who I was, which gave birth to a rigidity in how I approached living and even the path I created with my first encounter with cancer.

With the initial diagnosis, I gave full authority to my traditional doctors, a traditional drug therapy, and fear. During this time, I proceeded clinically through time and life. It would take a second discovery of this illness to fuse me with my heart and soul. The search within drew me to a path reaching the deepest caverns of my being. It was a remarkable awakening of my ability to hear the whispers of my inner voice as it guided me to who I truly am to be. Its precious gift: life; a full life.

Along the way on this incredible journey, I empowered myself with the responsibility that I hold in my healing, and I cherish the wonderful guardians who grace my life. I am a different person; a better individual; a more awakened soul. My realization now is the knowledge that I will forever sojourn with the cancer and that my healing will need my attention and compassion until my last breath.

It is a voyage that continues, but it has enriched my life in numerous ways. Thank you for being part of my journey and gracing me with this presence in yours.

Michael W. Kovarik
2013

The Journey Begins

The real journey of life aims at revealing something essential and original within us.

Michael Meade

I can still recall that cloudy, chilly January day as I made my way to the surgeon's office. The week before, I had minor surgery to remove a lump located in my left chest. I had discovered the lump months earlier but had ignored its warning signs out of fear.

At my yearly physical, my general practitioner, Dr. Kelleher, suggested I go to a surgeon to have the lump removed. I, feeling the brunt of my fear, replied, "Let's just give it some time." My doctor, continuing the physical, mentioned that it was most likely a cyst, for it had many characteristics of one. Dr. Kelleher went on to mention how he and his fellow physicians were beginning to hear about male breast cancer. I hesitated and let my fear override his suggestion.

After a few months, I noticed that my left nipple was inverted. It was then I knew deep down that something was wrong. I made another trip to my GP, who in turn sent me to a surgeon, who removed the lump. Now here I was, waiting to hear the results. Friends had suggested I have someone there, but I didn't see the necessity. "Why?" I said to myself. "It's only a cyst."

Well, there I sat in his office on that cold January morning. The doctor's deep voice garbled in the background as my body and mind responded stiffly to his words. "Michael, I wish I had better news."

Then it came: the C word. Cancer. I was stunned, dazed, stripped of any reaction. I sat there motionless, hearing only bits and pieces of the doctor's explanation.

"The lab report says it most likely originated from your chest and lungs."

"What?" this frightened voice inside of me screamed. "I quit smoking twenty-five years ago! How can this be?" This terrified voice within, quaking and stammering, went on, shouting, "This is a cyst!" Yet no one heard that hollow cry.

My doctor continued talking as I maintained my denial. As his voice became clearer, I heard him say, "My gut is telling me that you are one of those rare cases of male breast cancer."

I was numb. *Male breast cancer.* Those words echoed inside of me. *How, when, why?* The words hung above me like a dark cloud, obscuring any ability to see what was in front of me. My head was spinning, releasing a stream of tears that flowed uncontrollably. This was not how I wanted to begin my fifties!

As our conversation was coming to its conclusion, the surgeon gently instructed that I was not to leave his office before calling my general practitioner. He graciously left the room to give me some privacy, as my fingers numbly punched in my GP's number.

Between my sobs and tears, dear Kathy in my family doctor's office spoke tenderly. "Michael, Dr. Kelleher wants to see you today at 4:00."

I nodded in reply, as if she could see me. Finally, I was able to push out the words, "I'll be there." I gathered my things and left the surgeon's office. I sat in my car and let my emotions come.

My good friend Peter accompanied me to my GP's office that afternoon. I was still in the midst of raw emotions, disbelief, and wondering how this all came to be. My doctor, on the other hand, was fully prepared.

"Michael, I agree with the surgeon that this is most likely breast cancer. But I have been treating you for over eighteen years. Something else would have surfaced to give us the belief that this originated from your lungs. Just to be sure, I have you scheduled for a chest X-ray tomorrow. I have also looked up surgeons who are familiar with this type of cancer, and I am going to hook you up with an oncologist who I feel is the best. She is currently not taking on new patients, but I will call in some favors."

This wonderful physician continued speaking to comfort me. As I sat there, for the first time that day, I sensed that I was going to be okay. A feeling of comfort, although minute at the moment, was present and began to grow. I knew I was in good hands, and the solace took a firmer hold.

I quietly drove back to my home with Peter and his partner, Chuck, there to support me. They stayed with me for a while before traveling back home. I retreated in the solitude of my abode, my sanctuary, for I was exhausted and emotionally drained. I struggled to grasp this reality as fear set in once more. For the first time, my own mortality was facing me, and it wasn't welcome.

On January 24, 2007, my journey began.

The Gifts Begin

Even the thought of giving, the thought of blessing, or a simple prayer has the power to affect others.

Deepak Chopra

At home that evening, I set about making phone calls to let family and some friends know of my circumstances. Each person I spoke to was taken by surprise. Support was given with words and heartfelt emotion. Their calls went out to others after we spoke. At the time, I was unaware of the many gifts this journey would present, but it began that evening as my phone continued to ring. Friends and family called to console, support, listen, and love. I realized at the end of this long, emotional day that the first gift of my voyage was revealing itself. It was the support and love of the people closest to me.

This offering continued to manifest at work over the next two days. Because my doctor had set up a chest X-ray to confirm his belief that the cancer did not originate from my lungs, the next morning, I quietly went in to work to schedule a substitute teacher to teach my third-grade class. The few people who knew of my situation came to see me and wish me well. After completing the plans for the substitute teacher, I left to have the X-ray and then headed home for the day.

Sensing the need to be home for another day, I went back to school the following morning to complete additional plans for the substitute teacher. Word of my cancer diagnosis had traveled quickly throughout the building. Colleagues came to find me to hug, comfort, care, and cherish. I was truly amazed and overcome by the response. People went out of their way to locate me and provide support. As I prepared to leave the building, I was overwhelmed by emotion as I realized how much these individuals cared for me.

Approaching the exit, I crossed paths with a young teacher who came out of his room and asked how I was doing. Honesty poured out of me as I vocalized my fear and how deeply moved I was by everyone's reaction. He thoughtfully looked at me and in complete sincerity remarked, "Mr. K., you have no idea how loved you are in this building."

His words embraced me like a loving hug from a dear friend. Humbled and touched, I quietly walked to my car. My heart was warm. The gift of this journey was setting root.

I spent the rest of that day on the couch, my head heavy and crowded. My mind was frantically racing from thought to thought. The intensity grew as the day progressed ever so slowly.

To this day, it still astounds me how events occur and we miss piecing them together until much later. It is like a puzzle whose scattered pieces lie waiting patiently, eagerly, to be put in place by someone to make the object whole. I was still not in the emotional or spiritual place to arrange the pieces together and become whole. I had not yet awakened to the potential of the universe, this compassionate higher power, and my soul as they presented opportunities to do so. It would take some time. Unknown to me, I had a great deal of learning to acquire before the mystical magic of my healing was to sprout and flourish.

Throughout the day, I lay on my couch, at times strong, but mostly apprehensive about what was to come. That evening, the phone rang, and on the line was a voice I had not heard for twenty years. Tish, a dear friend and former teaching colleague in Virginia, spoke to me like we had last seen each other yesterday. I was stunned and overjoyed. We spoke for some time, catching up on the last twenty years.

She told me about her life, how she was currently in Nebraska, taking care of her father, who was ill. I listened to her news but did not share my news of the cancer diagnosis in that conversation. I know now that denial was still present. It was as if I was desperately hoping this was all a dream, one in which all would be back to normal when I awakened. We ended our call, promising to keep in touch.

I lay back on my sofa and wrapped myself in a blanket for comfort and protection. It was my way of keeping out the bad. As I settled within the warmth and safety of the blanket, my cell phone rang. On the line was my GP, asking me how I was doing. I was barely able to respond. Fear came rushing out as if a dike had burst, weakened from the force of the water it was holding back. No longer confined, this liquid, this fear, was effortlessly pouring out and covering everything in its path. I felt my breath retreating back inside of me, frantically searching for cover and safety, desperately seeking higher ground.

My doctor was calling to give me the results of the X-ray taken two days earlier. He didn't want me to worry or focus on the wait. I held my breath for protection. Dr. Kelleher joyfully shared that the results were negative. This meant that my lungs were not involved.

I could feel my breath escape and my rigid body slowly release its hold, yet I was silent, unsure of what I had heard. He was thrilled and wanted to share the great news. Words of thanks suddenly flowed out of me. After I hung up the phone, the tears began to appear. I let them stream out until they were ready to end. I caught my breath and made calls to family and friends to share the wonderful news.

As promised, my GP was able to hook me up with the oncologist of his choice. Dr. Janet Garguilo—Dr. G., as I fondly called her—was like an anchor one needs to keep from floating away. Her calm voice, caring personality, and gentleness grounded me at a time when I desperately needed grounding.

At our first visit together, Dr. G. serenely informed me that I would require additional surgery, a mastectomy of my left breast. I recoiled at the mention of more surgery. At the age of fifty, the only other time (other than the recent removal of the lump) I had been in the hospital was at the age of five, to have my inflamed tonsils removed. I was now going in for another operation within a few months.

Within a week, I met my new surgeon. After reviewing my case, Dr. Hena then discussed the mastectomy procedure. The surgery took place at St. Peter's Hospital three short weeks later.

Once again, I waited for results. Unfortunately for many of us, the waiting is when your mind travels to places you just don't want to be. And away I went. It is truly amazing the power fear has when we give it permission and free rein. Somehow I maintained my sanity until the follow-up visit.

A little more than a week after the surgery, I found myself in Dr. Hena's office once again. As he was thoroughly explaining the results, I was on edge. Dr. Hena reviewed that the cancer was contained in the lump removed earlier, and although the margins were good, there was one area where it was close to the edge. He went on to share that it had not spread to the lymph nodes or the tissues near the area where the lump was found. I eased back into the chair and breathed a sigh of relief that seemed to originate from my core. As it pushed its way up to freedom, I prayed it would take all of the cancer cells with it.

Another visit with Dr. G., and more plans were discussed. I was put on a drug called Tamoxifen. Then our conversation centered on another strategy. It was here that Dr. G. brought up the plan of my having radiation or more surgery to remove my left nipple. I sat quietly as she continued to explain that the lump's location was close to my nipple, and with one of the margins close, the doctors feel that it would be to my advantage to make sure that the area of the nipple was free of any cancer cells. I proceeded to sit quietly while taking in this information. Dr. G. suggested that I take some time and think about this. My reaction was one of resignation. I had hoped that I was done. Just tell me what to take, and watch me up to the five-year mark. My mind was already in motion, bouncing back and forth. I had no problem with them removing the lump, the tissues—it was to get rid of the cancer. But this, this is my nipple! Radiation?

To say I was somewhat confused is an understatement. Comments from others were intriguing. "I would do the surgery," so many remarked. "It's just a nipple!" others would exclaim. *Just a nipple*, I would respond within. "It's nothing," some would announce. "*You* do it then," I would argue inside of me as I stood smiling at their comfort at my losing a part of me. That was it. I was losing a part of me, and it wasn't an easy thing to digest. This nipple has been with me since birth. I can't just let it go. My emotions were on high alert. At times, the inside of my head felt like the beach, pounded by powerful, crashing waves, leaving momentarily, only to return to drum out the peace. As soon as I would decide to keep my nipple, the thought of radiation—well, neither choice was very appealing. As I struggled within, I yearned for the chance to discuss this with another man. Another male breast-cancer patient. I did not know of any man who had been down this road. I was on my own with this. Confusion was becoming the norm.

I was unable to see the universe work its magic and provide guidance to ease the strife within. Once again, a gift appeared. One day, during this intense conflict season inside of me, I visited with my friend Peter and a mutual friend, Jane. This generous spirit shared with me her passage with breast cancer and double mastectomy. I sat spellbound, not wanting to be anywhere else but here, listening to Jane reveal her journey and struggles. She articulated reasons for the double mastectomy, the fright, the loneliness, the anger of letting go of a physical part of oneself, and the coming to terms with what will be. Jane's honesty and tenderness hit a chord within me. I, losing a nipple, am sitting here with this courageous woman who gave up both breasts to live a full life. For the first time in quite a while, I felt grounded. Gratefulness materialized. It initiated in my heart and found its way throughout my being.

It grew and strengthened as this loving, gentle soul opened up to her core to let me in and share in her journey. Things were in perspective again. I left my time with Jane with a sense of direction. I realize and treasure Jane as a teacher. My connection with her gave me the tenacity to face my fears, to look within, and to trust. The surgery was to take place in April.

Once I had made the decision to have the nipple removed, I carried on as best I could. It was a struggle, yet I also needed to be sure the cancer was gone. I wanted it out of me for good. It was this thought above all that I held tightly. This thought provided me the needed strength when fear would raise its ugly head. My surgery was scheduled during my school's April break. The morning of our last day in school before the spring recess found me on the computer, trying to put into our substitute-teacher system my request for a sub following our break; a few extra days to heal.

As I diligently focused on my task, a meeting was announced over the school's intercom. I, being the most non-computer-savvy person, sat glued to my seat, struggling with my duty to secure a sub. My teaching assistant, Laurie, came into the room and mentioned the meeting. She felt I should be there. With my disappointment blossoming, she patiently sat beside me to assist me with my task. Shortly thereafter, the school nurse entered and said that I was needed at the meeting. We made our way to the library, walking down the silent and lifeless halls. The silence was eerie and only intensified as we approached the library where the meeting was being held.

Entering the room, I was greeted with cheers from everyone there. I looked around at the smiling faces with astonishment. My gaze soon focused on the cranes. Above my head were these beautiful cranes, these precious origami creations, gracefully dangling from the library ceiling, their twirling presence a wonderful comfort. As I fully took in the scene before me, I became acutely aware that there were hundreds of these cranes adorning the room. I was in awe, speechless. It was then explained to me that since my diagnosis, my friend and colleague, MDS (Mrs. Delancey-Smith)—Veronica, or as we lovingly call her, Ronnie—had been working with the staff of this wonderful elementary-school community to create a thousand paper cranes. This was based from the book, *Sadako and the Thousand Paper Cranes*, by Eleanor Caerr. This moving piece originated from the autobiography of Sadako Sasaki.

The beautiful, emotional story of Sadako Sasaki comes from the Japanese belief that the construction of a thousand paper cranes is a symbol of good health. I stood in this room, astounded and emotionally touched in a way no words could describe. Standing there, staring gratefully at these cranes peacefully dangling from the ceiling, was breathtaking and comforting. Throughout this joyful gathering, many individuals excitedly shared with me that there were in fact 1,012 paper cranes. They all wanted to be sure that more than one thousand of these precious cranes graced this room, to ensure my good health. I thanked everyone, and although my kindred friend, Ronnie, was absent due to a broken leg, her compassionate spirit and restorative energy were firmly secure in this room and in my being.

As teachers, staff members, and PTA moms came to hug and wish me well, along with the wonderful presentation of a poem creatively composed by Debbie Strugar on the impending loss of my nipple, a genuine sense of peace took its rightful place inside of me. The warmth, caring, and love present in that room remained with me not only throughout that day, but during my upcoming surgery, and for each day since. The energy given by those caring souls and their cranes is at home in my heart permanently. This special gift of healing and love was and is embraced and cherished.

A few weeks later, I was given a small photo album, recording that caring event from a friend and colleague, Judy. So many times, even now, years after that special day, I browse through that book of pictures. I can still feel the warmth and good wishes of those who were there. It has become even more of a treasure, in that a dear friend and fellow teacher, Amy, is there. We were to lose Amy later that year to a brain aneurism. I took in the energy and genuine emotions of all who were there on that wonderful day. Even I, at the time, was unaware of the healing power present in that gathering. The lesson was not evident then, but it is now. The magic of the cranes graces my life each day. Their simple beauty caresses my heart and soul and reminds me of the omnipotence of each individual and their ability to be a healing essence in one's journey

Finding Strength

Fear is a natural reaction to moving closer to the truth.

Pema Chodron

Following the surgery, my emotions were everywhere. At the core was fear. Questions raged in my head: *How will this look? Who will want to be with me physically?* My mind once again went to those dark rooms where doubt has its grip. Unfortunately, I let myself become a resident in these dispirited quarters within. It was a familiar pattern that I was accustomed to in troubling times. Though the bandages covered the results of the surgery, they could neither hide nor diminish my terror.

We live in a society where physical appearances take precedence over everything else. Our looks are us. Just listen to people as they size someone up. The conversation will most likely center on the individual's body, clothing, and status. How often do we tune into others' spiritual presence, kindness, or inner beauty first?

So there I was, looking at my physical state and wondering how another human being, especially a gay man, would see me. I had struggled with body image all my life, and now I was facing the removal of bandages that would uncover a body disfigured by surgery and cancer. Fear and anger took a firm hold of me.

When the day arrived to remove my bandages, I found myself stalling. Throughout the day, I found any excuse not to find the time to dislodge the bandages. I became very adept at discovering a multitude of activities I could be doing.

But once again, the universe came knocking. One of my avoidance tactics involved talking to friends on the phone. It was during one of these evading phone conversations that the universe let me know it was time to face the music. It wasn't a hit over the head or an accident where the bandages came off on their own. No, it was a breath of strength. Where this energy came from and how it appeared, I did not know, but it came knocking ever so gently.

Michael W. Kovarik

I was in the midst of a chat with a friend, and a quiet feeling came over me. It released itself tenderly and gradually swelled to a point within, until I knew it was time. I told my friend Sue that I needed to call her back.

I remember hanging up the phone and walking slowly to my bedroom. I eased my body down onto the bench at the foot of my bed and faced the mirror over my dresser. I sat there for a few minutes in complete silence, gazing at my reflection. My heart was pounding as if it were trying to release itself from my rigid physique. My entire figure began to quiver, not with excitement or anticipation, but with antipathy for what was to come. With hesitation, I gingerly took off my shirt, stood up, and closed my eyes.

Breathe

Balance begins with the breath.

Dan Millman

"Breathe," I told myself. I stood there silently, stiff like a soldier. "Breathe," I whispered again. Slowly, to give myself time to amass the strength I was looking for, I opened my eyes. My hand trembled slightly as it moved cautiously to the bandages. Carefully and steadily, I began the emotional task of removing them one by one. As the last dressing released, I closed my eyes. Fear was defiantly poking its head up to protest this brave undertaking.

"Breathe," I repeated. I could feel my emotions bulging inside of me, yet something held me together. When the tail end of the lone bandage liberated itself from my skin, I took a deep breath and slowly opened my eyes.

I glanced in the mirror and saw myself. "There it is," I said in a soft murmur. I caressed the area that was now without a nipple, surgical stitches taking its place. Tears formed in my eyes and were soon flowing down my face as I tenderly stroked my left chest.

In time, the tears subsided, and I sensed I was able to move on. I carefully put on my shirt and ventured back out to the living room. After sitting for a few minutes and contemplating what had occurred, I picked up the phone and called my friend back.

As I related my actions, Sue was thrilled. I appreciated her support, yet I could not feel that level of ecstasy. Even though I felt pride in what I had done, fear was present with its hollow voice echoing, *"Who will be attracted to you?"* Those toxic words bellowed to all fibers of my being.

"Breathe," I reminded myself as I valiantly struggled to regain the balance within.

Crossroads

*Our fate will bring us to a crossroads each
time we need to transform ourselves.*

Michael Meade

I was unaware of the power the negative voice inside possessed over me and its obstruction to my healing. As the days and months that followed the surgery brought me closer to summer, the conflict inside me intensified. With my body slowly healing, I continued my daily struggle with my new physical differences. It was not only the missing nipple but the noticeable difference in the structure of my once-symmetrical torso. Body image can do serious damage when we give it the power it hungers for.

During the spring, I went about my life, trying to create some sort of normalcy. Yet there was this continuous strife inside me. Even as gratitude for living through this disease unveiled itself daily, it was not enough to end this draining battle.

It seemed no matter how hard I tried, I could not escape this dreaded disease called cancer. That May, my mom was diagnosed with breast cancer, found in the left breast—just like mine. I desperately tried to keep my head above the swirling emotional waters. As my mom prepared herself for surgery, I aspired in vain to adapt myself and be there emotionally for her, but denial had taken root inside me and was vigorously spreading its noxious tendrils. I did not want to deal with this. I wretchedly wanted, I yearned, to be done with cancer, yet it kept revealing its aggressive face.

My mom came through the surgery with flying colors and embarked on the prescribed radiation treatments. She went on fully living, not allowing this illness to sidetrack her lifestyle, while I continued my daily struggle and denial. The bond between us of mother and son now included cancer. I was in a place of refutation so strong and emotionally exhausted that as she moved forward, I remained stuck in neutral.

During this time, my dating relationship was also in a state of transition. Although special, this connection was experiencing the growing pains of two individuals both at places in their journey where differing life paths were beginning to arise. Luckily, I was able to spend time with friends and try to concentrate on my healing. One Saturday, I took a ride up to a cottage in the country to visit some friends. While there, we decided to walk the rural roads to get some fresh air and exercise. As with many walks, it provided the wonderful opportunity not only to take pleasure in the natural surroundings but to enjoy the company and intimate conversation of friends.

Walking along the quiet country roads, I shared with my friends Patrick and Lee the situation I was in with the person I was dating. I explained how fully I understood where this individual needed to go in life, and how this relationship was also bringing up so much of my own baggage that I needed to confront.

Patrick, listening with his heart, remarked on the positive attitude I seemed to possess amid all the upheaval and asked if I was familiar with the work of Louise Hay. Not being acquainted with Ms. Hay, I asked Patrick to expound on her philosophy and writings. In that moment, Patrick's description of her philosophies overwhelmed me with its relevance to my life.

The core of Louise Hay's tenets is educating oneself on life's lessons. Patrick shared with me how Ms. Hay focuses on positive ideas and attitudes, responsibility, and affirmations that change our lives for the better. As we continued our discussion on this wonderful thinking back at the cottage, I heard a gentle voice within me firmly determine to explore this new realm. The day was drawing to its close, and I headed out. I knew before reaching home that I needed to purchase Ms. Hay's book.

That evening, I began devouring *You Can Heal Your Life*. The importance of this book and its life-changing voyage was something I was unaware of at that point in my life. Now, I recognize this day as the beginning of my true healing.

As summer graced my life and afforded me a reprieve from a work routine, I journeyed to a shadowy depth that I had never before experienced. That July, my relationship came to an end, and I learned that I possessed the BRCA-2 gene, making me more susceptible to certain cancers. I felt this illness was setting up a permanent residence within me. It became too much. I hit rock bottom; I was plunged into an emotional darkness I had never known.

During this troubled term, I read and reread Louise Hay's book. This wonderful, insightful gift became my bible and anchor. Magically, each time I perused this intuitive edition, I gained a different, more powerful knowledge and understanding of me. A deeper belief of the enormous power I hold in my healing was born inside me. This revelation did not surface immediately, yet in my initial reading of this book, it shed a comforting light that continued to grow during those dark, ominous days.

Once more, the universe patiently stepped in. While conversing on the phone with my friend Peter one morning, a gentle nudging within told me to reach out for help. I heard and understood its message and ended my conversation. Without much thought, I walked to my bedroom and retrieved a business card from the top of my dresser. This card, which contained the name of a counselor, had been given to me by the school social worker at the beginning of my cancer journey. This precious gift sat on my dresser where I had placed it months before, waiting for me to meet Cory, an individual who was to be a key in my healing. I could not at the time vocalize what inspired me to pick up that business card, but reflecting back, I firmly believe this was guidance that came from my intuition, my inner voice, my guardian angel.

By this time, I had reached bottom emotionally in my day-to-day challenge with the darkness that fully enveloped me. At that moment when I reached out to Cory, I began another part of my journey. This was a gift I was graciously giving myself. It was an offering that was to open parts of me that for so long I had locked up and ignored. I was desperately searching for how to cope and find my way. In that miraculous moment, I was oblivious to the doors I was finally to unlock and unaware of the freedom and healing that were to be revealed. Slowly and diligently for the next nine months, I empowered myself to shine and eventually leave the darkness that had engulfed me for too long.

With the darkness subdued, I continued to face the reality of the difference in my chest. Not knowing how to rectify the physical structure without invasive surgery, I focused on the missing nipple.

I met Dr. Rockmore, a plastic surgeon in Albany, and we discussed the possibility of nipple reconstruction. As the doctor explained the procedure and how the reconstructed nipple would look and feel, I knew I had to do this. Each morning, as I looked at my chest in the mirror, I was taken by the difference. The missing nipple was just that: *missing*. I longed to feel whole again. I felt this would help with my yearning for wholeness. I had the surgery in September and was now the proud owner of a new nipple, yet something was still missing. There was a dull feeling I couldn't negotiate.

On January 24, exactly one year following my diagnosis and the beginning of my journey with cancer, I was in a car, on my way to a tattoo parlor. Traveling with me were my friend Sue and a new person in my life, Tim. We were on our way to Seaville, New Jersey, to have my reconstructed nipple colored by a tattoo artist named Diane.

Diane travels to the Plastic Surgery Group's office twice a year, in the fall and spring, and performs magic and healing for women who have dealt with breast cancer and reconstruction surgery.

I had decided that I wanted to have my reconstructed nipple tattooed exactly one year after my diagnosis. Since it was the middle of winter and Diane would not be in the Albany area, I spoke to the plastic surgeon about my desire to have this done on the twenty-fourth of January, and he graciously provided me with Diane's number. I contacted Diane and shared my determination to have my nipple tattooed one year after my diagnosis, which I believed would help me come full circle. She listened to my story and offered to come in on her day off to help me complete this dream. So there I was on January 24, 2008, sitting in Moonlight Tattoo, having my new nipple colored.

Once the tattooing was done, Sue, Tim, and I drove to the shore. Here, in the midst of a January snow squall, I watched with pure joy seeping from my heart as Tim collected seashells and Sue snapped pictures of seagulls with her cell phone. Covered from head to foot to keep out the frigid cold, I stood smiling at the importance of that day.

In the span of that one year, I had four surgeries. I did rise out of that exhausting year stronger in many ways than before the journey began. It was a year filled with many emotions. There were numerous hurdles to overcome, doors to open and some to close, new individuals to welcome and embrace, and others to part with—yet all of this can be seen as gifts to my healing.

With the discovery of a lump, an important and life-changing journey began and continues.

Denial, Learning, and Searching

*Study the prison you have built around
yourself ... by inadvertence.*

Sri Nisargadatta Maharaj

Following my trip to New Jersey, I settled into a routine of work, family, friends, Tamoxifen, and doctor visits. I was asked by the Capital Region Action Against Breast Cancer (CRAAB), an organization in the Albany area, to write an article on my experience and journey with breast cancer. The time I spent composing this piece was extremely therapeutic. The emotions that arose during this time of reflection were intense and needed release. It was common as I was writing to have tears flowing as I recalled certain events during that year of journeying with cancer.

While writing this article, I became acquainted with the dedicated women involved in this wonderful organization. Their caring, love, support, and strength have helped numerous individuals deal with this disease. It is an honor to be part of such a compassionate, healing association. The phenomenal work they have done and continue to do has enabled many women and their partners to survive this journey with cancer.

My own healing was moving along, yet I was still struggling. I have to admit at this stage I believed I was done with the cancer. I believed that I just needed to take my Tamoxifen, see my doctors, and focus on the five-year mark, and all would be well.

During this time, my relationship with Tim grew, and soon we were searching for a place in rural Washington County. A suburban New York City boy, I had always dreamed of living out in the country. As we spent time traveling around the county, searching for that wonderful homestead, I continued my inner journey.

I proceeded to absorb Louise Hay's book. It was a godsend, for inside of me, denial and avoidance of my cancer were taking a firmer rooting. Ms. Hay's book enabled me to keep these negative forces somewhat in check. I diligently worked on forgiveness for actions, hurts, anger, and perceptions I held toward my family, friends, and colleagues, yet I was not able to look within and forgive myself for those same elements I strived to exonerate in others.

I had perfected this stoic, unified, and immense barrier around myself. Each time I read *You Can Heal Your Life*, I began to chip away at this self-imposed prison. Slowly, ever so slowly, the wall would lose a small part of its outer structure. My visits with Dr. G. continued, and I seemed to be on my way to that five-year mark and remission. I was on the right track—or so I thought. I was unaware that lurking inside of me, biding its time, was a darkness fortifying itself to eventually diminish my progress.

In September 2009, my dream came true when Tim and I settled in an old farmhouse with thirty-one acres in the town of Greenwich. At home, I eagerly set about exploring the fields with our dogs, Polar and Macy, designing and planting gardens and working on the house. All the while, I carried on with what I thought at the time was my healing from cancer.

My life revolved around numerous doctor visits: every six months with Dr. G., my oncologist, who now integrated a mammogram of my right chest as part of her therapy; yearly physicals with my general practitioner, Dr. Kelleher; and now regular visits with a gastroenterologist, Dr. Choma. With the discovery that I possessed the BRCA-2 gene, combined with the fact that my dad had passed away from pancreatic cancer, Dr. G. was determined to set up a program to check my pancreas regularly. With Dr. Choma, I now received a yearly MRI and an endoscopic ultrasound to assess the status of my pancreas. I felt covered in all areas. These talented and caring physicians were another gift during this time.

As the days passed, I began a daily struggle with the Tamoxifen. I became resentful of the pill and its negative side effects. Each morning as I popped this drug in my mouth, the pill itself reminded me of the cancer I wanted to leave behind. Realizing what was transpiring, I furthered my reading of Louise Hay's book and explored another one, titled *Gratitude, a Way of Life*. Each night I would share, acknowledge, and rejoice in my gratitude for all the people in my life and for my health following the discovery of the cancer. I was truly grateful for all that I had in my life, yet something was amiss. On the outside, I was happy, grateful, and full of life;

but inside, a different version of my life was brewing. Inside, I felt resentment of the cancer, its disfiguration of my body, and the pill I had to take each morning, which produced nausea, weight gain, and the loss of sexual desire. Each element on its own was taking a toll on me. Together, they were a force to be reckoned with, as I grappled with wanting to feel normal.

Inside of me, resentment and anger were progressively taking over. I kept up my reading, working on empowering myself with healing, searching within for the reason or reasons for all of this, and striving to be positive. I was aware of the gifts this journey had given me. I was a different person. I educated myself and believed I was doing all of the right things to keep this horrible disease at bay, yet something was not right. Again, I could not put my finger on it. My struggle and search continued.

The universe observed, it guided, it prodded, but I was not attuned to what it was saying to me. I had not awakened to hear its message or understand the soft nudging of my soul to see more deeply, to feel more deeply, and to trust more deeply. I now realize and acknowledge that the terror of this illness returning was embedded profoundly in my core at that time.

I am now cognizant of the fear's presence and its absolute power in obstructing one's healing. I know deep inside the wells of my being that trusting and feeling in your heart that the vacancy of this disease in your anatomy is when it is truly gone. The universe, in its wonder, was aware that I had not fully grasped my life's lesson. I was in the starting position, my engine revving, yet I was once again stuck in neutral. Something would have to encourage and, yes, force me to move beyond this fear I was holding on to. I wouldn't have to wait long for the universe to act.

Change

*A certain kind of courage is required
to follow what truly calls us.*

Michael Meade

The autumn of 2009 ushered forth the retirement of my oncologist, Dr. G. Our final visit in November granted me the opportunity to let this gentle individual know how she had touched my life, my heart, and my soul. Dr. G. was and will always be an anchor, a rock, a source of knowledge, a caring and tender spirit, and a healing gift. I will always treasure this special, gifted physician.

Change can be very frightening when we approach it with fear, the dread of the unknown. The power we grant fear is staggering. Yet this powerful emotion can propel us to discover what calls us to be who we truly are. Accompanying fear is courage, for it is courage that guides us to the path we need to travel.

My experience with fear led me to where I needed to be. As far back as I can remember, I have been uncomfortable with change. Yet, reflecting on changes I initiated throughout my adult life, it is both perplexing and amazing. I now see the universe's hand of guidance so present, yet hidden at that time.

I recognize now my being shy, introverted, and afraid of my own shadow was centered on my inability to accept being gay. The fear (there it is again) of others knowing, the rejection and judgment I anticipated were emotional responses I could not handle. I never felt that I was good enough. I empowered this thought. I gave it free rein to determine, judge, and convict who I was. The repercussions of this thinking were my emotional and physical distancing from family and friends. I wasn't comfortable with others knowing the real me. I kept running away—running away from myself.

The universe quietly stepped in. My running had actually elicited changes, which compelled me to grow as a person. It began following my attendance at a community college in New York; upon graduation, I chose to transfer to a large university in Pennsylvania.

Graduating from Penn State in 1978, I started my teaching career in a small town in New Hampshire. In 1981, due to staff reductions, I relocated to Newport News, Virginia. All the time, my running—which took me everywhere but New York—slowly stretched me as an individual.

My outer shell was beginning to crack. At this time, teaching was my life, for I was too afraid to have my own life. Yet this shell continued to fracture slowly even more with time.

It was in Virginia that I finally gifted myself the acceptance of being gay and began to emerge from my self-imposed prison. By 1988, I instinctively knew I needed to return home to New York. My running was approaching the finish line. So began my career near Albany, New York.

Now I smile and recognize the universe's guidance in this path.

But it would take a second relationship with cancer before my inner eyes, heart, and soul could merge; a second date that would press me to open more doors, confront the re-emerging darkness and the emotions stored so deeply inside of me. A place so deep in my recesses, a location I never imagined possessing the strength and courage to explore.

But then, the universe is capable of so much wonder!

The Opening of New Paths to Learning

Faith means living with uncertainty.
Dan Millman

Here in Washington County, Tim and I are surrounded by many wonderful and gentle souls. Our neighbors truly care about those who reside nearby. It is a special place to live because of the people who make up this friendly community. I was settling in this magical place and finally finding home.

The first Christmas Day in our home, we were invited by our neighbors, Sue and Tim, for a Christmas brunch. Sue and Tim are the team behind Spoonful Kitchen and Catering in Greenwich. Over the years, they have established a cozy tradition of gathering friends on this holiday morning to share laughs, good conversation, and delicious food.

In their warm and comfortable home, Tim and I met many friendly and fascinating individuals from the area. At one point, Sue shared with me about a yoga studio located in Greenwich.

Having a strong desire to pursue yoga for some time, I was thrilled with the news. Here was my chance. Sue told me about Zaidee, the yoga instructor, and where the studio was located. I was filled with excitement and couldn't believe my luck.

Within a few weeks of that gathering, my journey with yoga and Zaidee began. An immediate connection with Zaidee, her philosophy on yoga, and its effects in our daily lives took root. I was ready for its healing essence to become a part of me.

Being a novice in the practice of yoga, I enjoyed many occasions when Zaidee would share her background, philosophy, and beliefs on this mystical practice.

Zaidee began yoga as a physical activity. Loving dance and movement, yoga met her needs. As her practice matured, Zaidee tapped into the spiritual self. In yoga, as we align our body, less noise is getting in the way of our ability to concentrate, to quiet the mind, and to focus. It is this stillness and peace within that creates space for spirituality. We become sensitive to other things around us.

Our bodies, Zaidee believes, experience a sensitivity that allows us to heal. Over time, I too would see this peaceful path unfold, quietly fill the void within, and shed light on the darkness that was unfortunately becoming a permanent resident in my being.

Yoga is a valuable partner, in that it directly fixes one physically while opening the mind and the heart, making one more aware. Its flowing, rolling nature frees stress, enabling one to pursue or explore other holistic practices. We need to be more aware in order to open.

Yoga teaches us patience with time. In our world of instant gratification, patience, it seems, has been strewn to the sidelines. Yet it is the presence of patience that invites us to feel and experience the subtleties of other holistic conventions. For many, yoga is a gateway to patience, which in turn can be a portal to new paths in holistic healing.

I immediately embraced yoga. In time, the emptiness within began to diminish. Slowly, the void inside was being replaced with warmth and meaning. It was not only from the power and healing of this deepening practice; it also encompassed the many loving spirits drawn to this inviting setting.

The practice, the gentle souls, and the essence of this place were beginning to make me feel whole once more. I was home in the yoga studio here at Seventy Main in Greenwich.

Within a few months, my entryway to new restorative passages, in concert with yoga, would ultimately change my beliefs, actions, and direction in my own healing journey.

Yoga poses have the ability to open up emotions within, and I was experiencing that gift. Zaidee, knowing of my relationship with cancer, was very attuned to my practice and healing. Many of our conversations centered on alternative restorative practices like acupuncture and massage.

I caught myself hesitating to visualize my participation in these activities. I was content with my traditional medicinal path. Or was I?

Not being awakened to the power of these holistic practices obstructed my inner sight to their benefit in my healing. Yoga was wonderful, fun, opening. Acupuncture and massage were more personal. Fear of the unknown was present.

Sensing my hesitance, Zaidee, with ever-gentle reminders, kept these restorative paths in my sight and consciousness.

Over the coming weeks and months, those of us in the Wednesday-evening class cultivated a comfortable, supportive relationship and setting. I was full of gratitude for each of these special individuals.

Eventually, I discovered that Maud, one of the women in my class, was a Reiki practitioner. In our conversations, I learned more about this healing philosophy, theory, and practice.

One Wednesday evening, I mentioned to Maud that I was interested in a Reiki session.

It was easy to venture into this new healing practice because of Maud. She is one of those compassionate spirits with whom one instantly connects. The comfortable kinship Maud radiates draws you near and embraces your trust.

Maud's path to becoming a Reiki healer began with her son's massive head injury. As she sat with him in the emergency room at Albany Medical Center, Maud's maternal instinct and intuition drew her to place her hands on her son to reassure, to comfort, and to let him know and sense her presence.

The reaction was magical. There was a change in the electronic equipment, but more important was the calming effect on her son.

It was during her son's recuperation that Maud and her sister attended a talk on Reiki. The instructor used Maud as a participant in her demonstration. In the midst of the presentation, Maud realized this was what she had done in the hospital.

While immersing herself with this healing practice, Maud continued to work with her son.

Maud's belief in Reiki centers on the balance piece. It is the information she receives of a person's sense of balance, from the energetic body and one's spiritual body. It is what guides Maud in being a channel for healing.

Reiki involves removing a blockage or filling a void. It concentrates on energy flow, or lack thereof, in one's body. The connecting or intertwining of the energetic body and the spiritual was attracting and capturing my soul. I was beginning to grasp the core of this restorative practice.

Our first session opened my inner eyes to the magic of Reiki. As I lay on the table, Maud's hands traveled over and around my body.

There were times where the heat radiating from her hands was mystical, comforting, and restorative. I lay there in a relaxed trance, in total wonderment, marveling at Maud's ability. I felt a calming presence within. I found myself in awe of the generous power this healing work gifted my body, my mind, and my soul.

Our Reiki sessions now occur every three or four weeks. They are an integral partner in my healing journey.

During a session in early November 2010, something different transpired. Its importance was to be revealed later. In our session, as Maud concentrated on my back, she began to rub quite vigorously under the left shoulder. I thought nothing of it, as my trust in Maud was strong.

At the end of our therapy where we share and reflect on the experience, Maud apologized and explained about the rubbing. Her eyes gently looked in mine, and she described how the voice inside, her intuition, guided the focus to that area, where some blockage needed to be broken up and disintegrated. We spent time reflecting and felt it was most likely scar tissue from my cancer surgeries calling to be dismembered.

Within two weeks of that session I would realize how insightful the discovery of that blockage was to my health.

I was on my healing path, plodding along, and feeling all was well. I was doing yoga and Reiki; I had wonderful doctors, and of course, I was taking Tamoxifen. My focus was one of being positive and grateful.

So what could possibly happen?

At my next visit with my new oncologist, a concern arose. As my doctor conducted the routine physical exam, an area of the initial cancer surgery caught her eye. Uncomfortable with its appearance, she recommended an ultrasound be done.

I caught my breath with this discovery, yet felt things would be fine. Off for the test I went.

While the attending physician and nurse carried out the ultrasound, I was uncomfortable with what they were finding. As I lay on the table, I began reflecting on how tired I had been lately. I didn't seem to have the energy to perform tasks like before.

I attributed the tiredness to the long commute, my job, and trying to squeeze so much in on the weekends. Then I thought of my last Reiki session with Maud. What was going on?

The nurse gently continued with her positive remarks, but as I lay there, my gut spoke to me in a different tone. With the suggestion of doing a biopsy, tears appeared as this dark sensation within became more ominous. I felt it in my bones, my core. It was back. That damn cancer was back.

With the completion of the biopsy, the doctor, nurse, and staff were sensitive and supportive, yet guarded. I would have to wait for the results. More waiting. I thought I was done with waiting.

My mind became consumed with emotional thoughts. *How can this be?* an angry and terrified voice inside thundered. *All of these doctors, the Tamoxifen, all the positive changes I was immersing myself in. How? Why?*

I drove home to begin my wait. Tim was there for support, for comfort, and for presence.

The days that followed passed slowly, like the ticking of a watched clock. The Wednesday evening before Thanksgiving, I received the call from my oncologist. As I picked up the receiver, my breath became a prisoner within. Her voice said the words. *It is back.*

Even though I suspected deep inside, hearing the word *cancer* again in this context was a shock. It was déjà vu.

I sat at the dining-room table motionless, frozen, barely able to nod my head. I listened to my doctor's diagnosis and plan of action.

She would contact Dr. Hena, the surgeon.

I sat still, in surprise and resignation. I placed the phone back on its base and stumbled to the living room, where I collapsed into my favorite chair.

Arising within were my anger, my resentment, and my despair. Then the tears came. They were the key that unlocked my emotions and released them to freedom. My body heaved as the emotions poured out.

Sitting on either side of me were Polar and Macy, our Labrador/golden retrievers. They patiently, lovingly nudged their presence ever closer. I clung to them as my emotions flooded out of my being, releasing the anger and frustration that had built up inside of me. I held on tightly to these angelic creatures, for they were my anchor, my rock.

The gifted presence of these two adopted treasures allowed me to safely fall apart. They were there. They were love. They were support.

It is their loyalty, their deep affection, and their vibrant personalities that make me more human. They are my teachers. These tender living beings permit me to yell, scream, laugh, cry, jump for joy, and they are there. They are constantly and consistently present with their faithfulness and forgiveness.

Their magical essence, a gift.

In time, as I heaved the last vestiges of my fervent release, I took a deep breath for balance. I called Tim. He was on his way home.

Polar, Macy, and I took up our positions in the living room. The tears began to flow once more. I hugged these amazing animals and let my emotions fly.

As anger, fear, and frustration poured out of me I heard my voice ring out with strength and determination, "All right, Michael, you need to delve deeper. You need to work harder at locating the root of this illness."

The words hung in the room and echoed their message. This vocalization did not come as a surprise. With my reading of Louise Hay, I felt to my core that the cancer's return was more than my BRCA-2 gene or the environment. It was something within the depths of my being.

I knew I needed to be with this uncertainty, no matter how uncomfortable. I needed to trust this uncertainty. I needed to have faith in this uncertainty.

The next day, Tim and I were at my brother's home for the annual Thanksgiving gathering. I had privately shared my news with my mom, my brother, and my sister-in-law.

Sitting around the food-covered table and giving thanks, I sat there silently gazing at the souls present. Each individual at this celebration was an important part of my life; each an important part of my healing. I found myself engulfed with gratitude and love, and I sensed a healing being born.

My journey was approaching the path it needed to be on. This route would be unlike my first encounter with cancer, its gifts more potent and empowering.

Trust

Without trust, there is no peace.

Sri Nasargadatta Maharaj

A few days after the ultrasound, I was off to the surgeon's office. Dr. Hena's nurse and wife, Kathy, welcomed me like an old friend. Yet with the warm reception was an outward show of support and a heartfelt wish that my visit was for a different reason.

After I settled into an examination room, Kathy departed. Dr. Hena soon entered, and the familiar surgical discussion ensued. He reviewed the latest occurrences and set a date for surgery.

Once home, I sensed a need for a Reiki session. Before my surgery date, Maud was there for support. Her magical and healing touch was ever present. Calmness resided within every cell.

At the end of our time together, Maud gently announced that there were many "others" present in my home to assure and guide my well-being. My peacefulness and trust were heightened by this disclosure. I was not alone.

With me were Tim, my mom, our friend Sue, Polar and Macy, and the loving support of family and friends. I now was gifted with the presence of those no longer in the physical world. I embraced their spirit and felt protected and safe.

Inside, trust was allowing me to expand my horizon of acceptance to new experiences and beliefs.

My venture into Reiki has revealed a whole new realm to my consciousness. Trust tenderly caressed and exposed my mind to a new awareness. Its power, its extending peace, its loving healing was finding a stable home within.

At the time, I did not recognize or fully understand the potential of this new resident, its importance, and its solid base in my journey.

Trust was guiding me to a practice and secure belief in a healing path not only centered on traditional medicinal methods. I was slowly awakening to the empowerment of my true self and my true restorative path.

Many of its gifts were still hidden and unknown, but its peace and trust enveloped me. A warm, comfortable sensation pulsed throughout my psyche. It was like the comfort I feel when wearing my favorite flannel shirt; its warmth embraces me. I am safe.

The evening before and early morning of my surgery, I listened quietly and meditatively to Sue Van Hook's CD, *Prepare Your Body for Surgery and Recovery*. In the darkness of our living room, my body stretched out on the rug, Sue's gentle voice permeated my being. With complete calmness, I prepared myself and my body for the upcoming surgery.

I was ready.

On the morning of December 6, 2010, I was on the operating table at Albany Medical Center. I was back home the same day, back in Greenwich, where I felt safe and warm. This wonderful abode nestled in among the fields is my healing sanctuary.

I was home and, as my experience with Maud revealed, in the company of many spirits whose guidance and assistance was welcomed and treasured.

I was learning to trust.

Surrender

> *Surrender involves getting out of our own way and living in accord with a higher will, expressed as the wisdom of the heart. Far more than passive acceptance, surrender uses every challenge as a means of spiritual growth and expanded awareness.*
>
> **Dan Millman**

Following the surgery and recuperation, I gradually settled into a normal routine. Something inside of me gently voiced that I was okay. I began to trust this voice.

As I went about my daily life, I could hardly begin to visualize the twists, the turns, and the new paths my healing voyage would entail. Each day, my focus was on what I needed in order to further my healing.

I became acquainted with new authors like Caroline Myss, Dan Millman, and Deepak Chopra. I delved into their enlightening insights, thoughts, and beliefs on how to heal.

I began to empower myself in this medicinal journey. My awareness of the many teachers who were crossing my life path with their restorative and healing practice expanded.

In January, I was to begin six and a half weeks of radiation. I would no longer need to take Tamoxifen. I was overjoyed with saying good-bye to the drug, but this jubilation was not to last.

Since the discovery of the second cancer, my doctor had been in contact with numerous medical professionals, searching for a treatment path. Their conclusion and hers was to start me with the drug Lupron.

Lupron is commonly used by men dealing with prostate cancer. It is a leprolide depot injection, given once a month for the first three months, then one shot every three months thereafter.

At my surgical follow-up visit, my oncologist informed me of the plan to use this drug. As she thoroughly explained the reasons, I sat speechless.

"Michael, we don't know what to do with men where Tamoxifen hasn't worked and there is a reoccurrence of the breast cancer," she revealed.

Then she shared the descriptions of the numerous possible side effects. Tears gathered in my eyes. The emotions inside churned like a stormy sea. I heard this voice raging within: *No! No more of this. The cancer and that damn Tamoxifen have taken so much of me away! No!*

I sat glued to my chair, frozen. Tim, sitting across the room, observed my reaction. He could sense where I was going emotionally.

My oncologist, recognizing my uneasiness and difficulty absorbing the vital information she shared, graciously excused herself. After she exited the room, I fell apart.

"No," I heard myself plead out loud. "No, I'm not doing this. I've lost so much of me already."

Tim calmly and compassionately embraced me and asked, "Michael, what else are we going to do?"

Wow, with the release of those words, I felt as if I had run into a wall. *What else can I do?* I anxiously thought to myself.

I sat there hoping, praying that another plan of action would miraculously appear. But it didn't.

The wall around me was becoming taller, more solid by the second. It surrounded me like a prisoner. I was trapped, unable to move or even see beyond this budding immense fortress.

My head fell into my hands in despair.

"Why don't they know what to do with men who have breast cancer?" I quietly voiced in resignation.

My doctor returned, and I reluctantly agreed to start the drug. While she explained the process with the injections, I sat still, numb, the numerous side effects wrestling within.

Trapped.

My decision to take this drug was to be a phenomenal turning point in my healing journey, its empowering lessons to become clearer in the coming months.

The first injection was given in late December. Side effects emerged within a week. It started with hot flashes that unveiled themselves with a vengeance. One minute I was fine; the next I was sweating profusely.

This was not appealing to my third graders or me.

Sharing this effect with colleagues, I received from many of the women in my school the sentiment, "Welcome to my world."

I was not amused. Even with my compassion and understanding of the plight that so many women in this situation faced, the truth was, I did not want to be in their world.

I wanted my world back. I desperately wanted my normal pre-cancer life back. That old, familiar struggle was resurfacing. Once again, I was grappling to get myself back.

It became a daily mantra and challenge.

Anger was amassing its forces inside. Battle lines were drawn. I felt it brewing and heard its cries summoned in frustration.

I would get angry or upset at the smallest of things. Patience had packed up and moved to safer territory. My mood changed from one moment to the next. Not knowing what set it off, I felt trapped. The prison grew stronger, more furious with each day.

Anger, like fear, has the potential to steer one in a new direction. The emotion of anger, a gift from the universe, eventually would propel me to follow my heart. A magical insight within was beginning to stir. Awakened by the battle cries, it would need a few more nudges before I was to hear and feel its presence.

In time, I would learn to listen to this mystical protector who patiently waited to be acknowledged.

I contacted my oncologist's office, pouring out my journey with the side effects. Questions were gathering at the speed these repercussions were taking hold. "What else would come and take root inside?" I wondered.

My doctor's nurse contacted me that day and related their suggestion on prescribing an additional drug to deal with these effects.

Now I would be on two drugs.

I took a deep breath and then proceeded to inform her that I did not wish to take another drug to undo what the initial drug, Lupron, was producing in my body. Her response was that they recommend the new drug in conjunction with the Lupron.

Standing ground and subconsciously listening to my inner voice, I refused the additional drug.

I was beginning to discover the power of my inner voice.

As January approached its final days, the hot flashes and mood swings fully established themselves. With each new day, they fine-tuned their effect.

Wanting company, these unwanted visitors were now joined by a frequent need to urinate. I was waking up almost every hour on the hour with hot flashes or the necessity to visit the bathroom.

Over time, these nightly interruptions were taking a toll, for the lack of sound sleep produced an exhaustion that was draining the life out of me.

At school, I was dragging. Up at 4:00 in the morning, leaving the house by 5:45 to be in Albany by 7:00 for radiation treatment, followed by a day teaching third grade, and then the commute home. I was a walking zombie.

Colleagues and friends voiced concern on how exhausted I looked. I kept my focus on reaching the end of March. My radiation therapy would be completed, thus freeing up morning time. It would get better then.

Well, maybe.

In one of the weekly consultations with my radiation physician, I relayed my struggle with the numerous nightly trips to the bathroom. He offered to prescribe Flomax.

With his suggestion, the endless commercials filled my mind. The visuals of men needing to locate and then rush to the nearest bathroom exploded in my head.

"Oh, no," I declared to myself. "I'm not there."

I took hold of my senses, snapped back to reality, and politely declined, explaining my strong desire not to take any more drugs. Dr. Doyle listened and respected this approach.

On I went with sleeplessness, hot flashes, multiple visits to the bathroom, mood swings, and no sexual desire at all. Man, I must have been a barrel of laughs to be with.

These toxic forces, on their victorious march, were conquering my defenseless body. I was suffocating. I was exhausted, frustrated, and angry. My quality of life was dissipating steadily.

Trapped.

During this intense struggle, I repeatedly exclaimed to Tim, "I don't want to take this drug! I can only imagine what it is doing to my body." This anguished outcry occurred daily.

I was more frustrated, more exhausted, and angrier with each passing day.

Following one of my daily pronouncements, Tim, who was patient and supportive, remarked, "You know, Michael, it scares me when you say that, because what else will we do?"

I sat there with no immediate response. His words shocked me to a reality I had discreetly pushed aside.

Tim's intuitive comment hit me two ways. First is that I had been so consumed with this inner conflict, I had not taken into the realm of my consciousness what Tim was experiencing.

Too often, the partners, friends, and family members are on the sidelines, waiting to give support, yet unsure of how or when to bestow this reassurance.

We, the patients, are so often totally immersed in fighting, destroying, and dissolving this dreaded disease that we can be oblivious to the ones nearest us and their plight in this journey.

In marshalling up our forces to confront this intruder, we subconsciously blind ourselves to those in our immediate surroundings.

This is not done with disregard or lack of gratitude, but where all of our energy and passion is focused on healing. I was now more cognizant of the fear Tim lived with each day as he observed my strife with the drug.

Not knowing what my reaction might entail because of the mood swings, Tim had become uncomfortable in expressing his feelings. He was sidelined.

I, myself, could not explain what would set my emotions in action, what event or word might propel me to that dark place or what could bring me back to light. I sat across from Tim, respecting his fear, acknowledging it, feeling his love and concern.

The second effect of Tim's comment was of being stumped, unable to decide what else to do.

I felt like a river in winter, covered by thick ice, yet beneath the frozen surface, the current was flowing rapidly, churning, hidden from view. I looked at Tim and was unable to respond as to what we would do.

Trapped.

Within days of the eye-opening comment from Tim, I sensed a determination inside setting root—an observation point within, which originated from my core.

My inner voice, my heart was speaking, and I was awakening to hear its power of speech.

Frustration and anger were present, but now, so too were the keys to unlock the door to my inner voice of strength. This door, shackled for years, began to disengage from the chains that held it shut, thus granting my voice the freedom it yearned for and allowed it to be heard.

Its soft whispers fluttered from my depths and embarked on the journey it was meant to travel. I was now able to tune in to its sense of urgency.

But where do I go with this? What is the path to dissolve this struggle? What is my healing route if I stop taking this drug? How do I not succumb to this disease without a drug sustaining me?

Trapped?

In the early stages of our awakening, we begin to hear our healing voice. We are unsure of what to do and insecure about which direction to pursue.

Confusion and uncertainty are once again the norm. And it is confusion and uncertainty that elicit the fear driving our want, our demand, and our expectation for an answer right then.

But when we allow space for doubt and the unknown, a wonderful experience occurs. Our heart, our protector, our intuition will open, permitting the answers we hunger for to magically appear. They are tenderly delivered in a multitude of ways. These anticipated responses materialize in conversations with friends, family, and strangers. They enter one's soul through books, articles, and shows.

The final destination of these sought-after solutions is a permanent residence within your heart.

It is when we enter that uncomfortable place of desperation bordering on resignation that we finally surrender. I was in a venue where my spiritual and emotional status was in its infancy. Yet in my torment to unveil a new crossing in healing, I unknowingly surrendered to the universe.

Deep down, I wanted, I needed to trust that a more desirable path to heal was possible. I yearned to trust, not to be trapped.

With my act of surrendering, my heart, my soul, was unlocked to the guidance being revealed by the universe.

In this wonderful emotional state, I was unblocked to what was before me.

Allowing myself to enter and reside in this mystical space, I envision an open meadow on a bright summer day. Standing in this field, I stretch my arms out wide and take in the sun. Its restorative rays and warmth penetrate my body, dispersing its healing aura to every organ and cell.

It is a light of healing that shrouds my heart, my soul, my core. A feeling of purifying ecstasy engulfs my being, and I graciously accept it.

I am not trapped here.

Guidance emerged over the coming days. This gift gently let itself be known and with patience nudged me to a new path in my journey. The act of surrendering yielded a space open to new experiences and routes to heal.

Zaidee, my yoga instructor, had kept within our conversations the healing effects of acupuncture and massage. With the reappearance of cancer, frustration with the drug, and not knowing what else to do, I was more amenable to alternative or holistic practices.

My anger with the side effects was now the driving force in exploring new healing frontiers. The traditional medicinal method was feeling like an ill-fitting suit. It covered me yet felt uncomfortable. I was in need of a new healing wardrobe. Reiki was doing wonders, its healing and calming results evident with each session.

So on to more!

During the winter of 2011, I began my voyage with acupuncture. Zaidee recommended Bridgette Kinder of Ageless Acupuncture in Saratoga Springs.

On my first visit, I was instantly put at ease by Bridgette's tranquil personality. Her calming effect was reassuring.

Much of my nervousness centered on the involvement of needles. My present association with these pointed tools was at doctor visits—drawing blood and waiting for results. Fortunately, acupuncture would give me a new and healing relationship with needles.

In our first session, as I sat talking with Bridgette, my medical needle connection gently evaporated. I was drawn to this healing practice and instinctively knew I was where I needed to be.

In the coming months, as I opened to new holistic paths, the intuitive sense of being where I needed to be was a vital requisite in my pilgrimage to heal.

Bridgette's philosophy on acupuncture is that it allows one to drift into a place of different awareness. It is a space between awake and asleep. Here one can experience soothing visions and feel tension give way to free flowing of energy in healing and communication.

In Chinese medicine, the belief is that Chi is the life-force energy. Chi is our body's communication avenue. This thoroughfare is between every cell in the body, parts of the body, emotions, and mind. Chi is the illustrious facilitator. The communication is also a connection. The belief is that when one part of our body or mind is disconnected, then disease manifests.

Like yoga and meditation, which allow one to connect all parts that will promote healing, this space is present in acupuncture. The path within can be blocked by an emotional blockage, stress, phlegm, or heat. Acupuncture indicates what pathways to open first to achieve a healing response. The placement of the needle helps to unblock.

There are many factors to acupuncture that attract me, but it's the personal touch Bridgette gifts her clients that is foremost.

Our sessions begin with a conversation where I share what has come to light since my last treatment the prior month. Here, Bridgette will notice actions or physical emotional states that need attention. A cough, sinuses, bodily functions, and inner settings enable her to sense my physical and emotional status. As Bridgette carefully notes and negotiates from my sharing, she determines which points to use in attaining a free flow of energy. The treatment for that session may concentrate on my back, sinuses, sciatic, as well as my "maintenance points," which are employed in each visit.

With each needle placed at a specific point, I sense a release of toxicity and a corrective flow of energy. It is an energy flow similar to that in Reiki and yoga.

My belief in the connection between energy, energy flow, and one's health was deepening. I was entering a new medicinal realm in consciousness. Being uncovered was a vital part of my restorative path not considered in my traditional medical therapy. My awareness in noticing a more in-depth, emotional, and energetic force yearning for attention was unfolding.

I leave acupuncture treatments, like Reiki and yoga, in a very centered and peaceful state. It is a space that brings me to a healing where I have an active role.

It is the individual approach in each of these practices that is lacking in my present medicinal route.

There was a genesis of a subtle shift within. I was quietly moving in a more healthy direction.

Surrendering encourages quietness. I listened as my inner voice gave guidance to where I needed to be.

The internal wisdom of my heart was finally being heard.

Crossing Paths

Ultimately, each person holds the key to the story trying to be lived from within, but first someone else must unlock the mystery of one's life.

Michael Meade

Over time, with our move to Greenwich, Tim and I connected with a pleasant assembly of welcoming souls. It was among this gathering that Felicitas Anderson emerged and graces my life in numerous ways.

My fervent connection to Feli, as many of us within her inner circle call her, does not reside only on her angelic actions. Felicitas's vibrant, intuitive personality, her German accent and love of baking are reminders of my German grandmother. Our association is tangible and is enhanced by Feli's selfless acts of guidance to new healers.

Felicitas is my guardian angel. It was she who opened my eyes and mind to other paths and healers.

Her loving act of lighting a candle each morning at 7:00 as I journeyed through my radiation treatments was a tender and compassionate gesture. This simple deed was very healing.

During the radiation season of my journey, Feli shared a book written by Meredith L. Young-Sowers titled *Spirit Heals, Awakening a Woman's Inner Knowing for Self-Healing*. I graciously accepted the book. Examining the title, my reaction was, "How is this going to help me? It is written for women."

Focusing on the cover, reading the intriguing endorsements, I stood there pondering why this book came my way.

Within, my voice of wisdom and guidance quietly pronounced, *"Trust."* The awakening inside was providing insight and strength to explore the uncertainty.

In this sojourn, I've acquired a deeper understanding that actions, objects, and people cross your path for a reason. Some remain permanently with you, while others are here for a specific time.

Our take on these connections is to be open and thoughtfully receive the gift or presence.

My inner voice, the wisdom of my heart, was apprising me of the importance of this gift.

I plunged into the book, relishing its content full of one's power and the grace of Spirit to heal. It became another wonderful companion to my bible, *You Can Heal Your Life*.

I was determined and focused on continuing to chip away at the self-constructed wall that kept me a prisoner to traditional medicine as my only comrade in dissolving the cancer. I was becoming equipped with knowledge of my empowerment to better confront this disease on my own terms.

Strength in the belief of a more holistic, humanistic path for my health and sanity was setting root even deeper.

Reading Ms. Young-Sowers's book's specific statements, phrases, and opinions directly spoke to my soul. Near the beginning of the text, Ms. Sowers writes an expression so true in its content, so on the mark with my journey, it resonated deep within. She writes, "We must consult our deep heart and right brain to know how we feel about the people we're approaching for treatment, for we need to choose people who are not only skilled, but who listen to us and respect our feelings and opinions."

I read this statement numerous times. With each reading, the essence of these formidable words voiced their importance.

Each word, thoughtfully pieced together, elicited a mystical power that guided me in the coming months as major changes occurred.

I delved into a multitude of books on healing, the spirit of each consumed passionately. Unable to locate books on male breast cancer, I gained valuable insight reading of the many valiant women who courageously dealt with disease and paved new paths to heal.

Their words and raw emotions in their stories on healing from a variety of illnesses, shared by them and authors like Caroline Myss, Louise Hay, Mimi Guarneri, and Meredith L. Young-Sowers, gave me a base to stand on confidently.

The words written were magical, significant, and intense. Words are powerful, in that they have the ability to destroy us if we permit them, yet they also have the astonishing capability to direct, guide, evoke feelings and sensations of healing, ecstasy, and so much more.

The words I consumed were finding a home in my core. They were golden keys, which were to unlock doors within, concealing many frightened emotions.

Their precious gift: empowerment.

There are times where I find myself in complete awe when individuals cross my path at a time when I need them. My introduction to Dr. John Hearst of Pownal, Vermont, is one of those instances.

One Saturday in February, Tim and I were at a gathering in the home of our friends Peter and Rob in Hebron, New York. While enjoying their charming home set in the woods, my path crossed with John's.

The universe was in full action.

Felicitas approached me to talk. During our conversation, she thoughtfully remarked, "Michael, you need to go and meet John over there. He is an energy doctor."

Once again Feli reprised her role of guardian angel. It is a unique privilege and gift to be in the presence of one who guides you to where you need to be.

Eventually I found my way to John. The instant ease and comfort I felt drew me closer. I related my journey and received one of his cards to take home.

This connection was another forward step in my healing passage.

During the week following the gathering, I contacted John. The day of my first session, Tim, a friend, Sue, and I traveled the fifty minutes to Pownal, Vermont.

John and I spent the first part of the session talking, sharing, and exploring new depths in healing. Through this conversation, John tuned into my energy, goals, spirit, and physical being.

It is where much internal information is revealed.

Following the in-depth discussion was an evaluation. John began to assess the integrity of my physical framework by observing specific physical movements of my body. Afterward, I lay on a padded table while John focused on applying a light-touch, hands-on evaluation and treatment.

Here, John moves to different areas of your body, tuning in, assessing energy and energy flow and its connection or disconnect to your spiritual being.

Tim and Sue were present during the session, and at John's suggestion, were meditating, sending positive energy my way.

At the completion of the therapy, John and I shared our feelings and findings on what transpired during my treatment.

Driving home, I was in a space of feeling centered. It is a similar comforting expanse felt with each session of Reiki, yoga, and acupuncture. I was home with John's energy practice.

Reflecting on the similarities to these holistic therapies, the common core is one of inner peace. There was not a corresponding sense of quietness and calm with my traditional medical path. The discovery of a route immersed with inner peace and feeling centered was one I wished to pursue.

A new direction in my healing was being unveiled.

We were driving through Arlington, Vermont, on our way back to New York when Tim suddenly exclaimed, "Look out to your left!" Instinctively following his directions, my eyes fell on a wonderful sight. Effortlessly gliding above the waters of the Battenkill was a majestic bald eagle.

My eyes and soul transfixed on the natural visual. I'd never observed this powerful animal in the wild, and here it was, gracing us with its presence.

I was in awe and totally entranced. My eyes were glued to the magical creature as it flew above the river for a few moments longer and then departed into the distance.

Smiling and sitting deeper in my seat, I embraced the gift bestowed. The eagle, in its regal essence, is a symbol of health. A strong belief inside quietly whispered its message that I was going to be okay.

The whisper swelled in its intensity as I tuned in to my inner voice, my inner wisdom heart, my inner guidance, and heard its comforting message.

I shared my eagle experience with John and a close friend, Peter. At our next session, John gave me a written note exalting the needs of those with an eagle totem.

To celebrate the sighting, my friend Peter, his partner, Chuck, and a dear friend, CeCe, presented me with an eagle figurine, now at home in our living room.

These gifts are reminders of the healing, importance, and restorative presence the eagle's spirit has in my journey.

My connection with John spans two years of treatments once a month. Our conversations provide an open and thorough avenue to his philosophy on healing. With a background of more than twenty years as a family physician, John's medical evolution led him on a path to an integrative approach to energy medicine.

Deep in his core comes the intuition that spirit is our foundation. In his role as healer, John facilitates the connection between the physical and energetic.

As humans, we can feel disconnected from people or things around us. We shut down our connection through trauma or wounding. Often at this point, we need help, for our body truly remembers connections within itself and the outside world.

Our distraction is the physical realm. We are in a place of trying to remember who or what we are.

I was drawn to the tenets of John's philosophy and saw the connection between my inner struggle and the absence of my spiritual being. My inattention to its presence, its importance, and its needs was staring me in the face.

A key was entering the lock within and setting itself in motion to unfasten and dissolve the latch keeping my spiritual being hidden.

My evolving freedom and comfort in revealing more of me to John deeply enhanced the connection with my spirit. John has become a vital resource, healer, connector, and friend.

One day, in the middle of a conversation, I related to John my intense and emotional struggle with Lupron, its side effects, and diminishing quality of life. He compassionately listened to my frustration and churning emotions.

While he is uncomfortable telling someone what to do, his reply and insight were, "Michael, follow your heart."

Healing Within

Follow your heart, I silently repeated. Instantly a warm inner sensation took hold, and I knew my spirit was slowly returning.

These restorative sessions gift a connection where my physical being, my spirit, my heart, and my soul are one. I am emotionally centered and in peace.

Isn't that what we want and deserve with each doctor visit? For it is one's sense of peace and feeling centered that elicits healing.

Each visit with John, Zaidee, Maud, and Bridgette enable me to fortify my resolve and determination of a voyage in healing where I feel whole.

I am on the right path, yet aware there is more to learn, to confront, and to change.

At this tumultuous and exhausting juncture, I resolved to do my best with the destructive forces induced by the drug. I no longer wished to contact my oncologist's office where I would be told of an additional drug I could take for the symptoms my weary body experienced. I'd had enough.

I was now encountering pains in my groin area. At their onset, I would lie on my bed until they subsided. Curled up in a fetal position, my anger toward the drug and my belief that it was the only answer reached an explosive point.

I'd had enough of the intruder inside my body. This toxic tenant was affecting me physically and emotionally. I no longer wanted to be trapped in its tentacles.

My Spirit Speaks

*... listen to the intuitive wisdom of your
heart, where Spirit speaks.*

Dan Millman

While reading the works of Louise Hay, Meredith L. Young-Sowers, and Caroline Myss, I uncovered a connection with the vital link of one's spiritual being and healing. A few years earlier, my friend Ronnie had given me the book, *The Laws of Spirit* by Dan Millman. One day during this challenging struggle with Lupron, the book magically came into my sight. With an open heart and mind, I reread its pages. Spirituality, inner peace, and healing graced each page. Its message was one I needed at this time.

I had renounced spiritual realms since pairing it with religious dogma. Growing up Catholic and gay in the '60s and '70s, I desperately separated myself from anything religious or spiritual. I did not possess the emotional, intellectual, or spiritual maturity to understand the difference.

Now, as I slowly reclaimed my spirit and spirituality, the emptiness inside gradually began to dissolve. I continued to read various books and converse with Maud, John, and Zaidee on one's spiritual being and sensed an inner darkness being replaced with light.

The light was so strong, warm, comforting, and beautiful, its healing beams were settling deep inside. It was an internal light, enabling me to trust, to follow my heart, this inner voice, my spirit. This gift came peacefully in its own time, knowing I was finally ready for its presence.

It inspired me to live in the moment, in the present, and in a more meaningful way.

One morning, while getting ready to leave for a radiation treatment, one of my morning headaches arrived. A recent side effect, its intensity and pain were overwhelming.

I rigidly stood in the darkness of our bedroom, clinging to a dresser. My eyes were shut tight in the hope of minimizing the discomfort. Tim quietly asked if everything was all right. Eventually, through gritted teeth, I sobbed, "No. The pain is too much. I can't do this anymore. This is not living."

My body heaved as the emotions poured out. Tim came over and put his arms around me. I fell apart.

Exhaustion from not sleeping, radiation treatments, frequent and powerful hot flashes, mood swings, depression, pain in my groin area, no sexual desire, and now headaches were completely draining. I had reached the end of my rope.

I was no longer me.

Tim began to sense and see the drug's debilitating effects more clearly. Moving his fears aside, he realized things needed to change. But how? In which direction?

The further ascent of empowering myself in this journey began with my next oncology appointment. I fully respected the intellect and medical knowledge of my present oncologist, yet I had not been able to establish a comfortable relationship. There was always a distance. This disconnect was in total contrast to the comforting kinship enjoyed with Dr. G.

I was informing my doctor of the numerous side effects, when in the midst of our discussion, the doctor relayed, "I am not going to stop this drug."

I was taken aback. Immediately, frustration emerged, and then anger. The anger rose from deep inside. It was not feeding on fear but on the premise of not being heard.

My determination swelled, and I knew it was time to end the drug. Fear was relegated to the back seat, replaced by strength and trust. I left the office with a refined sense of direction and a deepening awareness of trust.

That week in my yoga classes, I was to encounter a sense of "me." It was the final puzzle piece, which had patiently waited to be placed.

The last ten minutes of yoga class is Savasana. After contorting ourselves in various positions or poses allowing emotions to seep out, Savasana is where one's body rests in a meditative state. Lying down or sitting, it is in this quiet mode that the body is calm and the mind still. In this spiritual abode, one can tune in and gently hear the heart, the soul, speak.

As I embraced the stillness and peace following a class where I struggled with each pose, tears suddenly emerged. Quietly, I let them flow. My body, my soul, and heart were sending guidance.

Discreetly, I wiped the tears away, breathed in slowly, and a voice inside eloquently stated, *I want all of me back.*

Understanding its vital message, my tears returned.

Savasana came to its tender close. Zaidee gently and spiritually guided us back to the present, to mindfulness. As we roused ourselves back, Zaidee quietly shared, "This special time can bring up emotions. It is important that we hear and honor them."

I realized she had noticed my journey during Savasana. My surprise transformed into gratitude and enlightenment.

I left class in peace. Inside, I was constructing my new path. It was somewhat cloudy, for the details and parts were not yet clearly visible.

The following yoga class presented the same spiritual experience during Savasana. Its message vividly repeated.

Driving the dark country roads home, I was unaware of the blackness but embracing the light within flickering with determination.

I now fully understood that the current traditional medicinal path was neither healthy nor the correct route for me. A change in direction was needed.

I yearned for a healing path where I was enjoying life, but more important was having all of me back.

Now, who can I talk to about this?

Making a Change

*Healing requires taking an action.
It is not a passive event.*

Caroline Myss

I needed to take some action. At my next session, John noticed I was at the end of my rope with the drug and its side effects. He mentioned knowing the oncologists at the Cancer Center in Bennington, Vermont. They were not holistic physicians, but they were receptive to working with patients who wanted to incorporate that path to heal. Would I be interested?

The universe, that wonderful higher power, strikes again!

The following week, John called the oncologists' office, which then contacted me. An appointment was made for mid-February. Things were shifting in this journey.

Between my session with John and my upcoming visit with the new oncologist, I had an appointment with my present oncology physician.

Prior to the scheduled meeting, I requested copies of my medical records. During the examination, my oncologist asked where the records were going. My response centered on the difficulty with Lupron and a quest to educate myself on possible options. In our discussion, some of the doctor's comments only enhanced my desire to explore other alternatives.

I left not angry but confident in pursuing a new path.

The fifty-minute drive from Greenwich for my initial meeting with Dr. Ives in Bennington found me in a contemplative mood.

Entering the Cancer Center building, I was greeted with openness and light. Within the structure positioned beside the waiting room was an atrium. The open, airy room permitted boundless amounts of sunlight to penetrate the space inside. The sun's restorative luster caressed my total being. From the abundant brightness, the plants, the colorful hanging quilts, I could not help but smile and feel warmly received.

While in the waiting room, you can gaze through the glass wall into the atrium, giving the sense of being closer to nature. Tim and Sue remarked on the difference from the other office. Both were enjoying the room's aura, its effect, warmth, and welcoming quality.

I was home.

Quietly moving around the room I took in its spirit. I noticed the usual traditional pictures displayed on the walls. Studying the pieces more closely, I discovered an enlarged photo of Dr. Ives standing beside one of her horses. Her natural smile was reassuring. The sense of being home grew stronger and more solid. This place was so *different*.

Since 2007, my sole focus in a waiting room was on diminishing the anxiety at what might come from the visit.

Would they find something? Would I be back to square one?

Memories, pictures seeped out of moments waiting for Dr. G., my radiation physician, my gastroenterologist, or my present oncologist. Waiting, anxious as I observed chemo patients slowly strolling by attached to an IV pole, shuffling from one place to another, their pole used as a cane, a lifeline.

Nervous emotions flooded out each time a name was called. As the patients rose to begin their time with the doctor, my eyes looked down as they passed.

A strange, unsettling reaction bubbled to the surface. I groped with the mind-set of why I was not subjected to chemo and its effects.

Survivor's guilt.

It is a guilt that erupted with each doctor visit where my focus, my thoughts, my being were totally immersed in a book. My eyes were glued to the text, not wanting to sense their pain, their fears, their discomfort, or acknowledge mine.

Eventually, I emerged from guilt's grip and was able to look at the faces of my brothers and sisters of cancer. We are a family.

I gathered the strength to see each soul with compassion as they journeyed with the disease. I wished them health, love, and in return sent these caring emotions my way. The guilt, the fear was replaced with healing.

Sitting in this new waiting room, I looked and smiled at those around me.

My healing was entering a higher stage.

Comparing the light-filled room with the windowless one of my present oncologist brought on a sigh, one comprised of emotions stirred by the comparison's meaning.

These memories, the differentiation was saying, *Look, Michael, take a good look around. Listen to your heart, your inner voice.*

My heart and inner voice were awakening to minute details of the room's tone and its positive effect on my attitude and emotions. It was recognition of this moment, and in this space I was at peace. With self-empowerment arose the courage to venture out and seek a physician who respected my feelings, thoughts, and experiences, which opened my senses to take in the complete surroundings. Take in not only receptionists, nurses, and doctors, but the inner essence of the physical structures, their message, tone, and the welcoming or unwelcoming features. Take it all in, for each element, each piece will enhance or stifle one's healing.

The importance of how I feel waiting to see the doctor, the interactions with office personnel and nurses construct the base for my visit and overall healing. A more intense focus is now centered on the significance, the relevance of each component to my time with a physician.

I sat in the well-lit room, feeling the positive, pleasant tenor of its space, the friendly receptionists, the cheerful nurses, all contributing in putting any concerns to rest.

With my name called, we were led to an examining room. Nervousness was present, yet somewhat contained, for my heart relayed, *You are fine. You are in the right place.*

One of the gifts from my current oncologist is the emergence of an intuition, a gut feeling of a physician's essence. Is it one of trust or one of disconnect and discomfort?

I've become acutely aware of this vital element. Thinking back, a sense of trust was immediate when meeting Dr. G., Dr. Hena, and Dr. Choma. I sat quietly, remembering my initial meeting with my new gastroenterologist. Upon entering the examining room, my instinct, my inner guidance, sensed Dr. Choma's spirit. I knew I was in good hands.

But would I feel that today?

The belief in the gravity of one's relationship with the physician as an essential link to healing is deeply embedded. For healing to manifest, all parties associated in the journey have important roles and connections. A burgeoning awareness of responsibilities I hold in self-healing is partnered with the relationship to each physician.

If one of these roles or connections is not a good fit, the negative effect on healing is seen and felt. Even with the utmost respect I held for my present oncologist, I felt no connection, and I had no voice. The desired and necessary partnership was not existent.

It is like when you try to buckle a seat belt and as hard as you strive to connect the two parts, they do not fuse. You continue to force the pieces together, but with no success. You become frustrated and angry. Then you pause, take a breath, readjust, and try again. Finally the familiar click is heard, and you're able to move on. That is where I am.

It is not clicking. I am readjusting to get a fit.

The door opened, and Dr. Ives entered. Her bright smile, peaceful spirit, and cheerful presence put me at ease. I caught myself smiling back.

She welcomed us to the Cancer Center and then settled into a chair and began to share the information gleaned from my records. I listened intently, trying to read her, all the while comforted by her amiable voice and manner. At the conclusion of her insights, Dr. Ives asked for my discernment on the journey with breast cancer.

The words poured out as I shared the passage, from the first diagnosis in 2007 to now. Dr. Ives sat quietly, listening attentively, hearing each word and catching the emotions that clung to each verse. I spoke of my struggle with Lupron, its effect on my body, my psyche, my relationship with Tim, and others.

With a compassionate, intuitive sense, Dr. Ives allowed my words to fill, settle, and become part of her. At the close of my summary, she smiled.

I paused and took in a deep breath. *Here it is*, I nervously voiced inside. *What will she think? What will she say? Will it be, "Michael, I wouldn't do anything different." or "You're doing what you need. Don't change course."*

I held my breath, as if to stop the moment. Dr. Ives smiled and reflected on my input. "Michael, I am hearing that you are truly struggling with the drug. You are doing so many wonderful therapies, like sessions with John Hearst, Reiki, acupuncture, and yoga."

My heart was racing as I sat still like a bird perched on a limb, waiting for what might come next.

Then the voice inside rang out, *Wait, did I hear correctly? She did hear me. My words, my emotions were heard!*

I felt this warmth radiating from my heart, which was glowing from acknowledgement. Instantly, Meredith L. Young-Sowers's comments on those we approach for treatments and how we need not only their skill but their ability to listen and respect echoed inside.

My voice was heard.

I made the decision to return in six weeks. Dr. Ives said, "We will do some blood work for a base. Then you and I, Michael, will discuss when or even if you might be willing to try a different drug as part of your therapy."

The simple yet powerful words, "you and I will discuss," struck home. We proceeded out to the front desk to set up the next appointment date. My elation floated me out to the car. A smile had taken over my entire face.

But now I needed to compassionately inform my present (now former) oncologist of the change.

Saying Good-bye

... the wounds and the poisons we encounter in life can become the exact opportunities for bringing out all the inner medicines and making things whole again.

Michael Meade

I have never been comfortable confronting or standing up to another individual. It centered on the long-held belief that I am not good enough.

It was the crux of my shyness, the inability to find my voice, and obstructed the discovery of my true self and true life path.

The gifts from cancer are numerous. From the love and support of those closest to me, the caring guidance of doctors, the crossing of paths with healers: Zaidee (yoga), Maud (Reiki), Bridgette (acupuncture), John (energy), and the exploring and embracing of my spirituality, I was to acquire yet another gift, that of my voice—one rooted in compassion, not anger; a power of speech from the depths of my being.

An ascent to a higher stage in healing required a compassionate and respectful closure with my current oncologist.

It would have been easy to cancel the next appointment, state over the phone that I would not be returning, but I knew deep down it had to be face to face. My doctor deserved it; I deserved it. In my heart, gratefulness and compassion were summoned.

Gratefulness for my doctor's diligent observation and discovering the cancer. Gratefulness for the time, energy, and directive put forth in a plan of action following surgery, and yes, gratefulness for her direction with the drug.

My struggle with the drug was where anger and frustration evolved from negative emotions to positive actions. For the drug's debilitating effects set free an inner strength to pursue healing on my terms.

It is a route that I embrace, yet this path is not for everyone. For some, a healing quest may comprise the traditional physician-drug approach. If one's heart, one's inner voice of wisdom is there, then it is the correct path to follow.

My second struggle with breast cancer had me look within, search my heart, my soul, and my core for a restorative journey partnered with my specific needs.

As a classroom teacher, I continually strove to individualize the curriculum for my students. I retain that same belief and right for each human being traveling his or her own healing crossing. It is a passage that must meet a person's needs, opinions, and convictions.

It is my hope that the medical community begins to search deep within through observation, conversation, and respect, to determine if a medical direction employed is the best one for that patient. They need to hear, genuinely hear their patients.

Empowered with these beliefs, gratitude, and compassion, I set out for the appointment with my present oncologist. With strength, trust, and a clear sense of a desired healing path, I entered the doctor's office.

In the waiting room, my nervousness arrived. The old behavior thoughts echoed in my head: *Who are you to think you need to change doctors? The doctor knows best. Do you? You can't make a decision like this.*

The words intensified as my wait continued. My insides were churning. The thoughts pulsated like a blinking red light in the fog. It was there, yet shrouded in mist.

I took a deep breath, thought of my time with Dr. Ives, and initiated a gentle conversation with myself. I refused to give in to fear or doubt.

Trust was my partner.

Directed to an examining room, I kept on with my waiting-room meditation. When the doctor entered, I sensed a change. Asked how things were going, I described my challenge with the ongoing side effects. Then, beginning with gratitude for discovering the cancer, I began to share my intention to incorporate more holistic therapies in my journey to heal.

We had a pleasant discussion, filled with questions and answers. There was no trace of anger or arrogance with my decision to leave, but a genuine interest in the therapies I would be pursuing.

I experienced another side of this physician, one who was listening, one who felt a change. It was a compassionate, gentle parting.

The doctor graciously stated that her door was always open if I ever wanted to return. As she began to leave, she paused, turned, and said, "You know, Michael, I think it was on your second or third visit that this all began. I am sorry."

I gazed at this physician, this human being, with respect and gratitude and quietly remarked, "Thank you, but I believe that things occurred the way they were intended to." With this, she smiled and silently closed the door.

These final words were a healing, for we both spoke from our hearts; a gift bestowed to each other.

Compassion and relief rose from deep inside as I sat down and took it all in. Sitting still and silent, I listened to my breathing for a few moments, gathered my things, and walked quietly out of the building.

I am grateful for this individual's presence, for she was not only my doctor; she was my teacher.

The lesson was to listen, hear my heart, my inner voice, my intuition, and I did. By empowering my belief in where and how my healing is to flourish, it established a home in my core filled with trust.

I began to trust, love, and believe in myself more each day. Its intensity grew, crowding out the belief of not being good enough, which had greedily consumed the space within, leaving no margin for spirit or trust.

With love, spirit, and trust strengthening, their aura flowed through my body, rejuvenating cells, embracing my being, and reviving my spirituality.

The precious gift of empowerment altered my thoughts and guided actions in nurturing the restoration of my soul. It unlocked the door of an inner, self-imposed prison, allowing my healing to soar and the release of courage to explore new, mystical realms.

Things were definitely shifting in my journey.

Exploring New Realms

> *... nothing is impossible when we follow our inner guidance, even when its direction may threaten us by reversing our usual logic.*
>
> **Gerald G. Jampolsky**

I was on a thriving path to restore my health. A wonderful offering of an openness to explore new mystical realms surfaced.

My friend and former colleague, Tish, assisted in this exploration. Tish forwarded the name of an astrologer from Virginia Beach.

With the second discovery of cancer, I was more than ready to plunge into and purge emotions deep inside. The insightful words that poured out in my living room following the oncologist's call in November were staring me in the face: "All right, Michael, you need to delve deeper. You need to work harder at locating the root of this illness."

These intuitive words nudged and guided me to a place of openness to take a risk with the unknown. My inner voice was saying to trust.

I e-mailed George, and upon his request sent the needed information of birth date, time, and place. The data was to be used in constructing a chart, giving a vision of my present situation. I was intrigued.

Within a few days, George asked that I call him on a certain day and time.

After the initial greetings, George began our phone session with questions concerning my parents. Since my dad was deceased, he focused on my mom. George prodded memories from childhood and then began sharing his insight and findings.

I wrote as he spoke, spellbound with the information shared, uncovering more of who I am. An understanding of why certain choices, actions, and beliefs were my base settled inside. I was a sponge, soaking up every last bit divulged.

It was awakening my soul, and I was transfixed with an emotional awareness never before experienced.

My whole body—its pores, cells, organs, and mind—were unhinged. It was as if my body was a parachute, yawning to its fullest ability, catching all in its path. It was not to slow down, but gaping wide open, inhaling, embracing to its utmost capacity.

My mind was racing, absorbing all George released. My head nodded in agreement and in wonder of the impact with each expression.

I frantically continued to record what George was delivering, "You as a young child ... ability to pick up unspoken feelings, emotions from your parents ... didn't know how to process this ... took on the suffering of those around you ... cancer ... not yours."

Entranced, I sat at the dining-room table assimilating, deciphering the particulars, and reflecting on their defining role in choices and actions made. God, I wanted more!

Engrossed in the dialogue, I wished George was here. I could observe his expressions, movements, and receive his tone more clearly.

George continued, "You need to let this go ... before the age of five ... feeling very unsafe because of picking up on parents' unspoken emotions and not understanding them or able to translate it all ... the little Mikey in you felt things were out of control ... he is going to leave ... little Mikey is the poet, artist, romantic ... loves to be in areas of unspoiled nature ... bodies of water ..."

I kept feverishly writing, copying down as much of George's revelations as possible.

George mentioned I needed to get in touch with little Mikey. He shared ideas on how to reach him, what to say, and how to speak from the heart.

I was silent and slightly dazed. It was not from overindulgence in this exchange, but from something else, something more defined.

It is similar to the moment when you connect characters, settings, and actions within a book. All the elements are in place, and a clearer picture materializes in your mind. It's when a refined impression of the story emerges. It's the a-ha moment. It is the placing of a piece of the puzzle on the path to making it whole.

I took the essence of this experience to heart. It was a key beginning to unlock the secured doors within. Over time, I was to unbolt more of these portals, flinging them wide open, realizing the fear residing there cannot hold me back any longer.

The releasing of memories, fears, and beliefs long held in the hidden canyons of my being, the umbilical cord of my draining illness, was to be an amazing self-loving, healing action. With their power nullified, their importance stripped away, and their presence banished, a heaviness carried for too long would gradually disperse.

The symbol I was born with, according to George, was that of control, and it went back many lifetimes. I was receptive to hearing the details on the connection of the past and its relevance in present thinking and experiences.

A determination in seeking out the root causes, the origins of the cancer, had me searching beyond the blinders I wore daily as I trudged through life. With this investigation, I kept in mind the simple yet insightful bumper sticker—*Minds are like parachutes … they only function when open.*

Well, my mind was certainly open, enlarging its capacity to see, grasp, and acknowledge ideas or thoughts not easily proven within our limited reality. I have the opportunity to hear different ideas and not immediately dismiss them, but allow them to be welcomed and have time to percolate.

They were a visitor who stays for a short time and then departs, bestowing their knowledge, connection, and healing requested in my journey.

George was ready to unveil past lives. I was ready.

In the first one, I was in the honorable position of a religious judge. I was a representative of spiritual truth in judgment, for I held certain doctrines or dogmas.

My amazement lies in seeing a present path centered on reclaiming my spirituality and its connection with a past life.

Coincidence?

George steered the conversation to reflecting on times in present life when I judged myself harshly or over a period of time. He expressed that I needed to look upon those moments when I was in fear of being judged.

Wow, where do I begin, and do you have a few decades to listen?

Both harbored unpleasant memories. I began to understand the base of certain behaviors, choices, and beliefs made in the present. The dots were being connected. A powerful emotional connection was unearthed. I was identifying a past life with the present and its impact on my healing.

George went on to share another past life where I was a military general. On the battlefield, I was in total control, never surrendering, never allowing myself to be emotional. I was tough, being strong.

I quietly laughed as George allocated these details. It arose from an emotional *wow*. It was such a contrast to today, with my difficulty making decisions where concern lies in how others will react and the ease of an emotional display in tearing up or crying at simple actions or events.

I did not see myself as tough or strong, yet I wondered what characteristics I might possess from the past.

As my journey to heal has matured, I have been in awe of a strength originating deep inside, enabling the life-healing changes made. I've discovered that in the midst of a life-threatening disease, the courage, strength, and the love we hold for ourselves comes forth. They surface when we are ready to marshal these powerful instruments and strive to heal.

Perhaps that general is there inside, part of my spirit, part of me.

My interaction with George was a positive self-education. It provided an insight into my deeds, selections, convictions, career paths, and self-worth. The melding of the past with the present afforded an appreciation, a grounded understanding, and tools to utilize in healing. My consciousness is alert and mindful of the choices, actions, thoughts, beliefs, and their positive or negative effect.

The letting go George suggested is done through journaling and visuals. I keep a journal, writing letters to those whose suffering and emotions I have taken on, to little Mikey, and recording daily affirmations. These written passages are where I reflect on their feeling unloved, alone, afraid, and how I no longer wish to possess the emotions and distress. The letters emphasize compassion and my ability to have the toxic emotions reside inside, unsure of how to translate them. As the sentiments became mine, their power

Healing Within

inhibited my cells, my organs, and my soul. Once firmly planted, they festered and multiplied in strength.

The passages to little Mikey were on love, support, letting go, and caring for his presence. They were an encouragement to leave the dark confines within and enjoy the light.

I clearly see the damage incurred by empowering the emotions taken on for their aptness weakened my spirit, presence, and health. Diminishing these intruders allows me to fully let go, enabling little Mikey to emerge gradually from the darkness.

With the letters, affirmations, and visuals, I began to let go of anger, resentment, and confusion. Each chipped away at the solid emotions.

The visuals took place in many settings. At times I visualized placing the noxious emotions onto a bird. Setting off, this redeeming creature carried the unwanted cargo away. As the animal steadily disappeared on the horizon, the growing distance between us pierced the heaviness and allowed a lightness to take its place.

Another favorite is where I secure these draining emotions in a trunk, place them in the basket of a hot-air balloon, and joyfully watch it float away. Peace gently swirls within, replacing the heavy load no longer present.

My affirmations are positive statements relating to emotions, thoughts, actions, and healing. With each written exercise, they become more secure as an integral part of me.

I continued consuming the writings of Louise Hay, Caroline Myss, Dan Millman, Meredith Young-Sowers, and Don Miguel Ruiz, striving to incorporate their teachings in everyday life.

It is a continual life skill, assessing the power in choices made where I favor practicality over self-nurturing. Feeling unloved permits the dark thoughts to fill my being, thus giving permission to the poisonous feelers to take root and set up residence. For it is with their habitation that my spirit departs, creating an ideal setting for the darkness.

I myself give them permission, so it is I who have the power to let them go.

Each day I chose to empower myself through reading, writing, reflecting, practicing forgiveness, and loving myself, the inner churning murkiness slowly disappeared. Its power diminished as I embraced new realms, new experiences, and mystical ways.

I hold on to the parting words George shared: "Michael, your past is not your potential, and your future must enter you long before it happens."

One day in early March, my friend Felicitas called, sharing the name of a doctor she'd seen. He was located in western Massachusetts and had come to know of him through a friend dealing with ovarian cancer.

Felicitas felt I might want to see him.

My first session with Dr. Lasneski of Alternative Healthcare of Western MA, Inc. was in April 2011. His background as a chiropractic physician with a master's in clinical nutrition and certified in botanical medicine spiked an interest in what he could offer in my passage to heal.

The core of Dr. Lasneski's practice centers on NRT (Nutritional Reflex Technique). It is a noninvasive muscle-testing technique developed by Dr. Lasneski, based on discovering possible causes of imbalance in the body.

In our initial discussion, he was very supportive of the direction I was pursuing along with my oncologist, Dr. Ives. Aware of Lupron and its numerous side effects, Dr. Lasneski understood my desire to stop taking the drug. Here was another individual who would share support, knowledge, and belief in my desired healing journey.

During the fifty-minute session, I sat on a padded bench in a variety of poses directed by Dr. Lasneski. At times, I would be holding a bottle or bottles of different substances while in a certain pose, as he and the assistant proceeded with their routine and observations. It was quite different from the other therapies, yet I knew it would provide another valuable perception.

At the completion of the therapy, Dr. Lasneski reviewed what he observed and recommended some supplements to take until the next visit in eight months.

Within this conversation, he asked if any of my doctors suggested a mastectomy of the right chest area as a precaution. The question caught me off guard, and I quickly responded, "No."

Driving back to Greenwich gave me time to examine the visit. The level of comfort with Dr. Lasneski was reassuring, and I felt he was a wonderful addition to my group of healers. The distance to home also allowed a reflection of his poignant question concerning a mastectomy.

My inner voice was in full action. *A mastectomy on the right side. Why? More surgery.* The words stung as they settled in. *Precaution? No! No more surgery!* The voice echoed with determination.

While silently contemplating the interesting method of NRT as the car plodded homeward, the need to look within at my reaction to the suggestion of surgery was taking hold.

The strong emotional response to Dr. Lasneski's words spoke of fear. A discussion with my oncologist was a must.

I had an appointment with Dr. Ives in late April. We reviewed the time between visits, and I shared my new connection with Dr. Lasneski.

Dr. Ives was supportive and interested in the work of this new healer. I relayed his comment about considering a mastectomy of the right chest area as a precaution. While sharing the comment, a grin appeared on Dr. Ives's face. I looked quizzically and asked, "What's up, Dr. Ives?"

With a voice tinged with relief, she quietly remarked, "Michael, I have been wondering all day how to broach this subject with you. I'm glad that Dr. Lasneski was thinking the same thing. You see, since you are not comfortable with a drug program, and even though the odds are small of the cancer spreading to the right side, I was hoping you might consider this as a precautionary action. Would you consider discussing this with your surgeon? We can call and set up an appointment for you."

With her words released, I gathered them up. I was smiling yet stunned.

Surprisingly, rejection of the idea did not surface. Having heard the suggestion from Dr. Lasneski, reflecting on my initial reaction, and now hearing it from Dr. Ives, I was receptive to the mastectomy. Trust me, the thought of additional surgery was not overly appealing, but having no interest in a drug therapy, well I was on board.

I agreed to see Dr. Hena, knowing if he felt the surgery was unwise or unnecessary, he would say so. I made an appointment, and in May, I was once again in Dr. Hena's examining room.

This time, it was different. This time it was my choice.

There I was, perched on the edge of the examining table, as Dr. Hena listened attentively to the idea of the mastectomy as a precaution and all that had transpired with me since the surgery in December. He took time to think about all that was divulged and in the end believed the surgery was a good idea.

With all of my doctors, including my GP, Dr. Kelleher, in agreement, my holistic healers supportive, and my strong desire not to do a drug program, I was comfortable with the decision to proceed with the mastectomy. The resolution was empowering, in that I was following my heart, my inner voice, not fear.

As the surgery date approached, a deep inner sense arose that the procedure would give symmetry to my chest. I was reluctant to vocalize the recurring body-image thought, wondering if it was vanity driving the belief.

Yet, many times since the cancer surgeries, the left-chest mastectomy, and lumpectomy, I've constantly thought and felt my chest was no longer proportional.

Catching my reflection in a mirror, I'd study my upper torso, observing an absence of symmetry.

Was it noticeable to others? I would deliberate this point over and over. Tim consistently reassured me that it was not, but deep inside, I felt it was. I saw the difference each time in the mirror, and it was bringing me down.

Now, don't get me wrong, I was extremely grateful for my health, a new path that was drug-free, and yet each day, following a shower or slipping on a T-shirt, I was more aware of an uneven appearance.

Silently, it was brewing inside. Not as intense as the body-image struggle endured most of my life, it was simply present and now coming to the forefront. It did not take me by surprise, but its present hold was very evident and in my face.

Since I had been intensely focused on exploring different avenues and thoughts in healing, this self-observation was kept in check, relegated to the back until now.

With the impending mastectomy, this silent concern was determined to move to the front of the line and firmly state its importance. Uncomfortable with removing my shirt, even in a doctor's office, the recognition of the effect my chest's demeanor revealed was now a conscious reality.

Knowing these thoughts and beliefs can negatively impact one's healing, I speculated on whether I was giving them permission to do so. Part of me dictated by societal views of the body still resonated deep inside.

The insight was a lesson to grasp.

Gradually, I came to a place where it was okay not to struggle with this. It was a reality, but I no longer wanted to fight its presence. For each time I gave it permission and battled its forces, this thought, this belief became stronger. I was gifting it strength.

In my readings, *not judging* was a returning topic and lesson. When you do not judge a thought or belief, it begins to lose its hold, its power, and its luster.

The bigger picture emerging was my yearning to feel and look "normal" again. Its definition was comprised of my own experiences and societal pressure.

The inner drama was quietly put to rest following a Reiki session with Maud. The day before the surgery, Maud announced at the end of our therapy a wonderful healing presence of "others."

This revelation helped clarify the unique experience I was encountering during the session. There were numerous moments when Maud was in the midst of her therapeutic touch and I felt the presence of additional hands on my body. For example, during our time together, Maud concentrated on my chest and heart area. With my eyes closed, I lay there peacefully, visualizing colors, favorite places, quietness, and I fixed on restorative sensations. I continued to feel a gentle hand placement and pressure on my chest yet sensed that Maud had moved on to a different part of my body. Gently, I opened my eyes and saw Maud positioned by my feet, but I still detected the existence of hands tenderly placed on my chest and heart.

I was still taking the comforting experience in when Maud added, "Michael, I believe you will feel more symmetry with your body following the surgery." I looked at Maud, not knowing if she had tuned in to this inner churning dilemma or had come to this conclusion on her own. Either way, it enabled me to share the struggle and the peace her thoughtful words evoked.

Feeling confident that the path unfolding was enhancing my healing, a tranquil warmth was present that evening and the following morning as I took in the CD's gentle tone and message on preparing one's body and emotions for surgery. I spent time thanking my right chest area, the cells, and the nipple for their presence.

On June 17, 2011, the right-chest mastectomy was performed at Albany Medical Center-South. I was home the same day, the proud owner of a tube protruding from my chest. It was to assist in draining the area where the surgery took place. The projecting manmade article was surrounded by bandages, hiding the absence of what was, until the operation, my remaining nipple.

I embraced the aura of home, its comfort, its coziness, its sense of sanctuary.

As the day wore on, a nervous thought of taking care of the surgical area, now including the tube, arose. A familiar queasy feeling surfaced. I closed my eyes and focused on my breathing. Calmness arrived like a welcomed visitor. "It will all work out," I gently repeated. "Tim, my mom, and Sue are here to help." I trusted once more.

The following day, I carefully observed the area where the tube exited my body. Sitting down during the exploration assured that if I were to pass out and fall, I would not end up back in the hospital. I chuckled, for in that moment, a wonderful, joyous sense enveloped me as I proclaimed the resolution with the end of an involvement with future surgeries and hospitals. This declaration produced the strength to examine my chest.

The memory of the left nipple's removal in 2007 flashed before me. I fell back to my tool of breathing. I sat quietly, closed my eyes, and focused on the breath.

After carefully uncovering part of the area and then gently securing the bandages once again, I knew assistance would be required to clean the surgical site.

"We'll tackle this later. Now I will just enjoy the day," I softly stated.

When evening approached, Tim asked if I needed any help with the bandages. I quickly responded, "Yes!" Up we went to the bathroom, where after unbuttoning my shirt, we slowly removed the dressing. As I gazed upon the tube protruding from my chest (securely held inside, I hoped) filled with red liquid traveling to a small container residing in my shirt pocket, I felt weak and instantly sat down.

"Breathe," I whispered. Tim took over. He cleaned the area and put fresh gauze back in place. After emptying out the liquid in the small holding container, attaching it to the end of the tube, I quickly placed it back in its necessary position, safe inside the shirt pocket.

Tim assisted for the next few days until I felt confident in performing the task independently without losing consciousness.

The first time I cleansed the surgical space on my own, it was a cherished accomplishment. It further cemented to the reasons why an interest in pursuing a career in the medical field never materialized. For your doctor or nurse to faint while performing a similar task would not be comforting. But here I was, rejoicing with this achievement. In this moment, I had scaled the mountain of queasiness and fear and etched another notch in my healing journey.

I couldn't wait to get the tube out. With impatience swelling, I carefully worked outside, weeding and planting flowers. Why waste a beautiful early summer day when the garden was calling? Being in the garden was therapeutic and great for the soul.

The handling and digging of the warm earth, the simple and healing delight in admiring the colorful plants and how they complemented each other with their distinctive hues all fusing together was enriching my spirit. I was blending and healing with Mother Earth.

While enjoying the needed time in nature, I was constantly checking the tube, making sure it was intact and secure.

The days passed, and finally I reached the point where the liquid exiting the right chest was at a consistent level in the container for three days in a row.

Off to the surgeon's office!

The day of my follow-up visit with Dr. Hena and the removal of the tube had arrived. Anxious and relieved, I followed Kathy into the examining room. My heart pounded furiously as the last vestige of my path involving surgery with this disease was becoming a reality.

Dr. Hena inspected the area, removed the few stitches attaching the plastic tube to my skin, and proceeded to draw out the tube.

Aware of my weakness in these situations, I lay on the table, closed my eyes, and clenched my teeth. Unfortunately, the clenching only made the procedure more uncomfortable. In this tense state, the process seemed to take longer that I had hoped.

At last, the discomfort eased, and I heard Dr. Hena's voice announce, "All done, Michael."

I let out a long breath as my body slowly released itself from the tension of that position. It was done!

I stood up, put on my shirt—which no longer held the red-filled container—shook Dr. Hena's hand, and left the room.

Passing Kathy in the hallway, we hugged a good-bye, and then I exited the building to head home.

On the drive to Greenwich, Tim shared that there was a good amount of the tube inside of me drawn out by Dr. Hena. I smiled for the times I was nervous and concerned that the tube might fall out.

Taking in the scenery of the Hudson River as we ventured homeward, a brilliant smile graced my face as I felt in my core, *no more surgeons*.

The days of summer were a time to recuperate, gain strength, and enjoy. It would be some time before I could rejoin my yoga class. For now, I focused on healing and smiling. Many friends remarked on how well I looked as the summer rolled on.

I knew this time I was done with cancer.

Delving into Buddhist Peace

If in our daily lives we can smile, if we can be peaceful and happy, not only we, but everyone will profit by it.

Thich Nhat Hanh

Traveling around Washington County in upstate New York, you will discover its beauty, its vibrant rural culture, and its friendly citizens. Agriculture is its main economic force, yet on a sunny September day, you may sight the brilliant colors and gracefulness of a hot-air balloon gliding across the sky, preparing for its participation in the annual balloon fest.

You will come across galleries and shops proudly displaying original creations by many of the artists who call this area home. The simple beauty of this county and surrounding areas will induce a calm and tranquil soul.

My amazement in residing in this aesthetic space is in its people. Diverse in experience, education, and politics, the farmers, cheesemakers, bakers, artists, and more grace you with sincerity and respect.

It is here that I truly found home and people who have become family. The vitality and spirit of this region has drawn healers like Zaidee, Maud, Bridgette, and John. It has welcomed so many of us from afar who cherish its comforting aura.

Our friend David Armbrewster is one of those welcomed souls. One day in late summer, David called, inviting Tim and me to be part of a small group, which would be meeting every other Sunday at his home in Cambridge, New York. He was starting a Buddhist study group and thought we would be interested.

I've always had an interest in exploring the Buddhist philosophy but struggled to pursue it on my own. This small-group setting was ideal.

In early fall 2011, a small group of us gathered in David's living room, sharing thoughts on what direction to travel. After a few meetings, we decided on a format where we would begin each assembly with a twenty-minute meditation, followed by an hour of discussion.

The conversation would be led by David, who had been part of a Zen learning group while living in Minneapolis, prior to relocating to Washington County.

The Zen learning group David attended while living in Minnesota was at the Clouds Water Zen Center, followed by his migration to sit at Common Ground Meditation.

Upon moving to New York, he has been involved with the Vermont Insight Meditation Center in Brattleboro, Vermont. This background made David the perfect individual to guide us novices on a learning path with the Buddhist philosophy.

One of David's teachers at the Vermont Center suggested we begin our journey with the book, *Insight Meditation,* by Sharon Salzberg and Joseph Goldstein. Every two weeks, we would meet, meditate, and then review and discuss the chapter read, centering on a specific meditation facet or thought.

My participation in this group has engendered a deeper understanding and respect for meditation and its healing effects.

In present-day life, I, along with many others, have become accustomed to rushing everywhere and through everything. We've grown into a culture and mind-set of immediate gratification and an immersion in stimuli. There is a loss of knowledge and experience on how to be quiet, how to enjoy a peaceful day without constant interruptions from phones, iPads, and computers. Somehow, we have misplaced the concept and joy of simplicity.

In my journey to heal from cancer, I have discovered a yearning, a need for simplicity.

This naturalness is present when I am alone in the gardens, planting, weeding, or designing a new bed. The only sounds are those of nature. For me, quietly listening and breathing in the cry of a red-tailed hawk soaring high above the freshly mowed fields; the gentle breeze encouraging a rustling of leaves; the determined crow of a rooster up the road; or the distant barking of a neighbor's dog embraces my heart and sets a tone of peace and stillness. These natural sounds invade my spirit, becoming a permanent healing.

Unfortunately, life and its hectic schedule can disrupt the consistency I strive to maintain with daily meditation and simplicity. But I have learned to just begin the routine again.

In my reading of various books on healing from an illness or disease, it is repeatedly stated how meditation and/or prayer as a vital restorative practice gifts the quietness, the stillness, and the connection to a peace we yearn to become one with to heal.

At first, I struggled with meditation, as I was unable to quiet the mind. Each time I sat to meditate, my mind would review interactions with others, emotions, and constantly project situations or events that hindered a still mind. I felt frustrated with failing miserably at a practice I desperately wanted as a path in healing. I sensed others in the study group were achieving the peace I craved from meditating.

One of the many wonderful offerings in the discussion piece of our gatherings was listening to fellow members share their difficulty in quieting the mind. I was brought back to reality.

David shared a few strategies with us. One was naming the scene, emotion, or actions occurring in the mind as you meditate. For example, quietly name the event going on in the mind as: "story," "anger," "fear," and then return to meditating. An essential part in naming is not to judge what is going on in the mind, just to name the experience. Another strategy was returning to one's breath. Here, without judging when the mind is wandering, gently focus on the breath. The attention on the breath quiets the mind and releases the emotions of anger or fear, which may be the root of the traveling.

I utilized these strategies at the group meditation and home. At times, I was successful, while in other situations, the story in my mind took on a life of its own, with intermittent periods of quiet. With a reliance on David's advice, a compassionate conclusion that this was okay eventually emerged. I was judging the traveling, and this in turn encouraged the wandering to flourish. Gently, I began stating, "All right, the quiet will grow in time. It is okay."

With practice, time, and patience, the quietness began to deepen.

The acquired ability to release judgment was freeing. Its liberation and tranquility spread to actions and thoughts in daily life.

I became aware of judgments made throughout the day with myself and others. Hmm, there's that judge from a past life showing up again.

It was an opening connection. Whenever I was mindful of judging, anger, or fear, I'd name it, and gradually it passed. Simply stating "judgment" or "anger" or "fear" summoned back the quiet. With the behavior becoming more consistent, more natural, I noticed a greater sense of peace penetrating my being.

The study of the Buddhist philosophy has replenished and reaffirmed my spiritual being. For so long, this void within, this emptiness was aching for fullness, for meaning, for substance. But until now, I did not have the faintest idea of how or what to fill it with.

For decades, I renounced my religion and religious core for its rigidness, hypocrisy, and isolation. I equated spirituality with religious dogma.

As an emotional and intellectual maturity burgeoned, I opened my mind, my heart, and my soul to new experiences, and spirituality arose from the darkness deep inside. I was able to digest the differences and realize within my heart that I yearned for my spirit to return.

In searching for new ways to heal, I recognized that the inner void was my missing spirituality. Slowly I rediscovered my spiritual essence through the books of Louise Hay, Caroline Myss, Meredith Young-Sowers, Dan Millman, Don Miguel Ruiz, and now those of Pema Chodron, Thich Nhat Hanh, and Michael Meade. I became a regular at Battenkill Books in Cambridge, New York.

The authors, doctors, and healers were my teachers, and I hungrily devoured all they shared. In conjunction with the study group on Buddhist philosophy, they were the incredible ingredients in a recipe to heal. I was slowly becoming whole.

I took it all to heart, and it became a permanent part of me. It was an integral facet of my DNA.

Just as important were the delight, support, and respect given by my doctors and healers for the rejuvenating path in reclaiming my spirituality. I received many comments steeped in wonderment from friends, family, acquaintances, and colleagues on how rare such a degree of support and respect forwarded by my traditional practitioners was.

A healing gratitude has taken up a permanent habitation inside. From what I observe and hear, this support and respect is a rare commodity.

It is a gift I accept and cherish.

The study group proceeded through the text, *Insight Meditation*, and I was taking ownership of a majority of concepts introduced. Yes, there were some that didn't resonate or take hold, but what I have learned in this journey is to embrace those concepts, thoughts, beliefs, and actions that speak directly to my heart.

The other convictions I hold aside to review or let go. My connection is to any action, thought, or belief that adds its healing power to my being, my spirit.

I continued to learn, explore, and discover with the Buddhist philosophy. I saw and felt its effects, yet I needed to delve even deeper.

The exploration began with Sharon Salzberg's book, *Loving-Kindness*, along with various texts by Thich Nhat Hanh and Pema Chodron. I was connecting to the philosophy unveiled from these authors that change begins with me. Peace begins with me. Respect begins with me. Healing begins with me.

When disillusion with society, our culture, and world events finds a home inside of me, I reflect and realize I only have control of my actions and thoughts. When frustration heightens with the lack of knowledge on men's breast cancer, I discern that my healing from breast cancer begins with me.

Actions of respect, peace, good health, and spirituality begin with us but possess the wonderful capability to interact and affect others. The way I choose to act, speak, think, and believe when originating from the heart can travel and embrace those around me.

During my exploring and enhancing of my meditation practice, I came across a loving-kindness mantra and instantly fused with its message. Its simple essence calms, centers, and focuses with intent and quiets the mind.

When I meditate, I quietly release to the universe:

May I be filled with loving-kindness.
May I be well.
May I be peaceful and calm.
May I be happy.

The gift of this poignant Buddhist saying is the capacity to add or change words or phrases to reflect an individual need or intent. The prayer's strength is that you begin with loving-kindness to yourself before graciously sending it to another.

I change or add words and phrases to mirror where I am emotionally or spiritually. I silently repeat the mantra as I sit in a doctor's office, at home, or in nature. These caring words elicit a sense of centeredness. When extending this blessing to another individual, I simply insert their name in place of "I." For example:

May Tim be filled with loving-kindness.
May Tim be well.
May Tim be peaceful and calm.
May Tim be happy.

This spiritual philosophy is a welcomed and cherished partner in my journey to heal within.

Psychic Connections

The spiritual journey involves going beyond hope and fear, stepping into the unknown territory, continually moving forward.

Pema Chodron

It is difficult, verging on impossible, to find a family that does not possess some level of dysfunction within its parameters.

Many of you my age (fifty-seven) and older grew up with TV sitcoms like *Leave It to Beaver*, *Father Knows Best*, and *The Donna Reed Show*. How many of us hoped, prayed, and wished upon a star that our family could be like the ones perfectly portrayed each week?

Reality shows us the impossibility, for a family is comprised of human beings. They are people who, at their best, make mistakes and at times reflect the behavior of their parents.

For me, the wake-up call came when I repeated a certain phrase to a student in my classroom. It was when one of the children kept asking why they needed to do a particular task. At a stage of frustration, knowing I needed to move on, and after fully explaining the sensible reasons (or so I thought) why, I stood there and looked at the eight-year-old and stated, "Because the words came out of my mouth."

My body froze as the voice within exclaimed, *Oh no, I sound like my parents!*

How many behaviors do we exhibit mirroring those of our parents, grandparents, aunts, or uncles? But if we stop, reflect, and learn where these actions, emotions, and beliefs originated from, we discover a family behavior pattern going back generations.

Without our acknowledgement, awareness, or acceptance of this, we produce our own toxic emotions and reactions in response.

Holding on to anger and resentment, we blame our parents or others for not recognizing their learning or acquisition of these emotions and behaviors. By subconsciously being a victim, it allows us not to assume any responsibility in holding on to the noxious elements. We then permit our spirit to leave, thus enabling the thoughts, feelings, and beliefs to have room to set up house within.

I was there. I held on to my anger, resentment, and beliefs and constructed an immense barrier between myself, my family, and my friends.

Now in the midst of this journey, I firmly recognized and believed that the retaining and empowering of anger, resentment, and fear held for so long is one of the root causes of my cancer. This enlightenment came through reading works by Louise Hay. It was the breast cancer, a major defining and terrifying disease, that was the catalyst in opening my eyes, awakening my soul, and exposing my heart to my responsibility in its development.

Was holding on to anger and resentment the only reason? No, but it played a defining role, along with choices made in nutrition, interactions with others, difficult situations, stress, and the environment.

The retention of anger and resentment was the paving that allowed cancer to be born, grow, and freely travel.

The gift from cancer was the altering of my take on things. With the second diagnosis in 2010, I embarked on a whole new path to heal.

I began to truly face my anger and resentment. Louise Hay guided my new direction with her words, "Resentment that is long held can eat away at the body and become the dis-ease we call cancer." Her statement resonated deep inside, yet I wondered, how do I release the toxicity from my body, my thoughts? Again I went back to Louise Hay, where she shared, "I have found that forgiving and releasing resentment will dissolve even cancer."

Forgiving sounded easy, but there are actions of emotional, verbal, or sexual abuse that are difficult to set free. In numerous books on healing, forgiveness is the core. It is the magical wand, the golden key, the light of hope, freeing anger and resentment. When I first read about forgiveness back in 2007, it was a difficult concept, as I struggled with the belief that by forgiving, I was accepting the behavior. Through the years, I kept working on forgiveness, using strategies Louise Hay shared in her books. With the cancer resurfacing in 2010, I plunged deeper inside, approaching forgiveness on a whole new level. Possessing an intense hunger to let go of the anger, the resentment held for too long, I gradually was able to release these emotions, setting them free by forgiving the individual, while not condoning the behavior.

The second diagnosis gave rise to an understanding of a personal responsibility for what happens to or within my body. It centered on what I believe about myself, how holding on to negative thoughts, hurts, beliefs, and emotions slowly destroys at the cellular level. This destruction welcomes disease and illness.

How I choose to respond to a given situation or conviction is that, my choice.

Have I perfected this behavior? Not at the level I'd like, for having this trait be consistent, it must be embraced, learned, and ingrained over time. A compassionate reminder is that the making of a mistake or reacting in an undesired way is learning. It may be frustrating, but it is reality. I continue to work at forgiving and not judging.

A constant refocus on choice behavior is called into action at times where I am off track, not centered, or feeling off balance. I rediscover the sources for my foundation by reaching for books by Louise Hay, Thich Nhat Hanh, and others.

The act of rereading these valuable texts is the universe guiding me back to retool, to grasp more firmly and intimately the healing characteristics of forgiveness. I immerse myself in Ms. Hay's simple phrase, "I forgive you for not being the way I wanted you to be. I forgive you and I set you free." It is used in forgiving others but also for self-forgiving. As with the Buddhist philosophy, where in order to extend loving-kindness to others, I must first extend self loving-kindness, forgiveness follows the same path.

It is an act of loving yourself, which is the core of all healing.

The exposure to various healers through their writings, thoughts, and beliefs gifted an awakening of my mind, my heart, and my soul. It connected me with the astrologer, George, and was the beginning of a new foundation in a mystic realm and healing.

In the midst of constructing a well-rounded healing base, my path crossed with a gentle psychic medium named Tracy Heller-Fluty.

I was introduced to Tracy by my friend and colleague, Karen. One late spring evening in 2011, a few of us gathered at Karen's home in Saratoga Springs to have a thirty-minute session with Tracy.

Since this was my first time having a reading, I was comforted with it being at a friend's home. We sat around the bar counter in Karen's kitchen, enjoying some munchies and drinks. In the midst of the conversation, I sat there wondering if anyone felt as nervous as I. The nervousness took me to a place of *What will I hear? Will it be bad or good? Was Tracy able to read my health status?*

My mind was cluttered like a NASCAR racetrack, with thoughts speeding in every direction. I looked around and noticed that everyone had brought pictures for their session with Tracy. Being a novice in this realm, I didn't think of bringing any. I was getting more anxious with each passing minute.

I took a sip of wine and focused on my breath. It began to work, and gradually the anxiety lessened. Some time went by, the conversation continued, and then in the background, I heard Karen's phone ring. Over the constant hum of voices, I could hear Karen saying, "Oh my gosh. Are you okay? Sure, we can do this on another night." Karen then informed us that Tracy would not be able to make it due to car trouble.

I let out a small breath of relief, yet I was also disappointed. Although fear was present, there was a distinct feeling that this path was one I wanted and needed to pursue.

Driving home, I took in the events of the evening and concluded that it wasn't the right time for me to connect with Tracy. I trusted the universe with this, yet I had an inner sense that we would meet and connect in the near future.

It wasn't until the following fall that Tracy was able to schedule another date. In the time between, I had gone through the right-chest mastectomy and recovery, begun a new school year, and was involved with the Buddhist study group. With pictures in hand, I was at Karen's in a more relaxed emotional space.

An apprehension was there too, but as Tracy arrived, a comforting feeling took root. We were introduced, and Tracy's genuine smile put me at ease. Any anxiety that had come along slowly faded.

We sat around the bar counter, listening as Tracy shared her path and background. Being a conduit from ones who have passed on to those of us here in the physical world, Tracy also touches upon our paths here on Earth. These paths involve careers, relationships, various happenings, and health.

After getting acquainted, Tracy went upstairs and settled in one of the bedrooms. It was here we would have our readings. My excitement was gaining speed.

Being the first to have a session, I gathered my pictures, breathed deeply, and began to proceed up the stairs. With each step, the noise from the kitchen sounded muffled and more distant. It was as if I was entering a new realm.

I walked into the room where Tracy patiently sat. Her bright smile and warm personality greeted me, helping to ease my body into the chair opposite hers. As I took in another deep breath, calmness became my partner and friend. Handing the pictures to Tracy, I told her of my interest in my career and connecting with my dad and grandparents who have passed. She sat for a moment and began to relate details concerning my career and possible future work. Then, after studying the pictures for a minute or two, Tracy connected with my dad.

She began by sharing personal events and people that only my dad and I would know. I felt his presence. As Tracy relayed my dad's feelings, tears gathered and gently started to fall down my face. It was a welcome release.

My dad started talking about a certain situation with a former student of mine. Tracy recited the facts conveyed to her, while I sat in awe. He stated that he was proud of me for the time with my student and how it affected her, proud of what I was doing, and proud of the man I had become.

Knowing how difficult this was for my dad to express while he was alive, it touched a deep part of me, hidden for so long. The tears flowed freely as he shared; he is with me more than I know.

But the most meaningful, most healing were the words my dad unveiled that acknowledged my path of forgiveness was indeed working.

Over the past few years in this journey, I have done a lot of work on forgiving myself and my dad for our strained relationship. I had attained the freeing realization, with assistance and guidance from readings on healing, that my dad was who he was because of the way he was raised. This awareness allowed me to forgive and begin to heal by loving him.

With tears cascading down, I heard Tracy's voice saying, "Of course I loved you. You've done a lot of work. Not proud of myself." Tracy interjected the image she was receiving of my dad with blinders on. His words continued to flow, "Breath … breathing … struggle … Heart was heavy … sort out my life … Son, this is how I was raised."

Peace. Its light-filled rays enveloped my entire physique at that moment. Those words were so powerful, so simple, so healing.

I began muttering between sobs, "I know. I know. I figured that out." A healing so deep, its intensity was melting away any cancer cells hiding in my body. Melted by the power of words I yearned to hear all of my life.

Melted by love.

While growing up, I had continuously strived for my dad's love and approval. I never felt I had it. Yet it was always there and at the best he was able to give or show it.

Since my emotional and spiritual awakening was in its infancy, I was unable to see or feel the presence of his love and approval. I wasn't able to detect their existence with eyes clouded by anger and resentment. Now, with eyes of compassion and forgiveness, I feel, see, and know of his love and approval.

In this enlightened space, bitterness is not welcomed, for there is no room for its toxic sentiment. An inner fullness was emerging, flooding my being with love, a love that was always there.

Tracy just smiled.

My grandmother let Tracy know of her presence. The first thing my grandmother stated was that she is with me more than I know. Like my dad, my grandmother is present in my life today. With this knowledge, I instantly thought of the additional hands I feel and sense during a Reiki session with Maud. It was a comforting thought.

Tracy reported how my grandmother enjoys watching me clean the house, as it has evolved into a time when I reflect and work through various personal situations. She laughs at how obsessed I am with making the bed each morning, shares her concern with the nausea and discomfort from the drugs, and is thrilled that my journey to wellness was going great. Tracy told of the visual where my grandmother was standing, holding a cake pan, telling of the joy she feels watching me cook.

Warm memories of times with my grandmother came flooding back. In the midst of these recollections, I was blown away when Tracy stated, "You are meditating now." Stunned, I looked at Tracy with total amazement, as this facet of my life had not been revealed. Finding my voice, I acknowledged that the practice was new to me, having only been with the Buddhist study group for just over a month.

Tracy laughed, imparting, "Your grandmother doesn't really understand it but loves it. She says to keep doing it."

I smiled, sensing the healing, which began with my dad's visit, continuing to blossom, spreading to every organ, cell, vessel, and expanse within my being.

With my thirty minutes coming to an end, I stood and hugged Tracy, thanking her for the powerful and healing gift.

Descending the stairs, I slowly re-entered the realm of present time. It felt as if I were floating, my feet barely touching the wood below them as I continued through the gateway.

All eyes were focused on me as I entered the kitchen. Everyone smiled, and my friend Ronnie exclaimed, "Michael, you are radiating! Your eyes are sparkling."

I smiled and quietly replied, "It was absolutely wonderful. I received such a precious gift."

Gently easing my body onto one of the stools, I grabbed a handful of munchies, poured a glass of wine, and sank peacefully into the seat. Inside, I heard the familiar voice shouting, "What a great evening!"

On the drive back to Greenwich, a deep sense of peace settled inside. It was the same essence of quietness that graces my whole self after sessions with Maud, Zaidee, John, and Bridgette. This wonderful group of healers has a new member, Tracy. As I glided along Route 29, the comfort of knowing my dad and grandmother were with me grew. I was not alone as I drove the dark rural roads on my way home.

Now, when reading at home, I occasionally shift my eyes toward the ceiling and smile, conscious of my dad and grandmother's company. Their enjoyment in watching me read—or as my dad put it, "watching you consume books"—is like being wrapped in a warm blanket keeping out the cold.

Tracy also shared that my dad leaves me signs that he is here. Appearing in the form of a bird, he is with me. When Tracy was communicating this fact, she repeated a few times about seeing the color blue. With the bluebird being my favorite bird, I sensed this was his signal.

After my time with Tracy I began to notice or become more aware of bluebirds around our home. The old barns and the wide-open fields are a welcome habitat for these graceful creatures.

With my spending more time at home, I continuously see my brilliant, blue-feathered friends near the farmhouse. As I gaze out the window, I observe them darting to and fro, momentarily perching on a limb to catch their breath and survey what is before them.

I take in their beauty, their color of blue sky, follow their antics, and catch myself saying, "Hey, Dad."

As My Heart and Mind Open, More Healers Enter

... yet our healing journey is all about change.

Meredith L. Young-Sowers

As my journey with doctors and healers continued, I felt a valuable and integral element was missing—one of nutrition. Although there was a realization of my emotional responsibility with the cancer, I knew from readings and conversations that nutrition played a major role in one's health. Mine needed to be refined.

Another change was knocking, and I was ready to open the door and welcome in the new.

Through my energy doctor, John, I acquired the connection to Maddie Sobel.

Maddie is a holistic health counselor who focuses on nutrition and its impact on the whole person. Certified through the Institute for Integrative Nutrition in New York City, Maddie was doing her sessions in Bennington, Vermont, where she lived.

Her gentle disposition, caring, and constant praise encouraged me to relax, dive right in, and embrace this new path. The respect and honor Maddie bestowed on any changes made, no matter how minute, was the support I needed to continue onward.

We usually met in the morning at The Bean in Bennington, which offered the opportunity to grab a coffee or tea, sit, and converse.

Each session incorporated new information, a review of my nutritional journey from the last meeting, and together developing realistic goals to focus on until the next time.

With Maddie, I was at ease and never experienced any judgment, which promoted total honesty about the food I ate, sampled, or was resistant to trying. The open communication produced an environment that welcomed change.

Our conversations centered not only on nutrition, but included physical activity, spirituality, stress reduction, and relationships. All play a crucial role in healing and good health.

In reviewing lifestyle changes and dietary practices, Maddie would diligently listen without judging, praise the changes undertaken, and offer practical suggestions to enhance the adaptations, so the new behavior became mine.

One of the first diet changes I instituted was eating kale on a regular basis. With Maddie's guidance, I combined foods of multiple colors, thus introducing a larger variety of nutritious sustenance in meals.

If you are like me and it is difficult to enact a diet change, Maddie's advice was to move slowly as the menu changed to a healthier one. The gradual introduction of new habits cultivated the adjustment to become a permanent one.

As with learning anything new, the ups and downs are there. By not judging and by compassionately directing the diet back on track, the healthy change materializes.

A heightened conscious awareness of how the body feels following consumption of certain foods is my guide to better eating habits and health.

The important missing link of nutrition was now a viable member of my healing, and I kept moving forward, connecting the scattered pieces of the healing puzzle. With each new piece added, an inner emotional and spiritual openness thrived. And it was this unenclosed liberation that welcomed new individuals and experiences.

The second occurrence of breast cancer and the horrific tide with the drugs were the magical key unlocking my consciousness, my inner voice and wisdom from the deep crevices within.

Their freedom removed the blinders inhibiting my spirit from detecting the diverse realms present in our lives. The openness, the unbridled liberty were my guides to crossing paths with yet another healer.

A shaman.

I came to know Carol Tunney through John, my energy physician. He was once again assuming the role as a pivotal connection to other healers. As John observed my explorations into a range of healing realms, he felt comfortable sharing about Carol, who was a shaman. Noting my trust and confidence in Maud (Reiki), Zaidee (yoga), Bridgette (acupuncture), Tracy (psychic), and himself, John was confident I would be receptive.

During a session in late winter, John spoke of his friend Carol and her healing practice as a shaman. My interest was immediate. I listened as John shared his knowledge of what Carol's practice involved. I was hooked. Not knowing much about a shaman, that afternoon I searched the dictionary for its meaning. The definition, although minimal, gave some insight. As I read of a shaman being a priest who uses magic for the purpose of curing the sick, divining the hidden, and controlling events, it sounded mysterious and piqued my interest even more. I needed to contact Carol.

Our initial conversation was pleasant and intriguing, as Carol shared how this path in assisting others to a new healing avenue came to be. She spoke about her practice, and I was instantly drawn to the therapy.

Carol recounted how this restorative path is one of the last modalities to be embraced. She went on to share how shamanic therapy is not much different from the other energy-focused work like Reiki or my sessions with John.

As a shaman, Carol's focus is more on the spiritual instead of the energy. She believes that all dis-ease or illness begins with spiritual disharmony or imbalance, and left untreated, it will trickle down to the emotional.

Her job is to restore to the individual the energy he or she has lost. The energy healing works, according to Carol, because energy is spirit is love. What she is actually doing is seeing the person's divinity and reflecting back his or her divine perfection and beauty.

Carol began to describe the layout of a shamanic session. At the beginning, we sit in conversation to establish rapport. This provides time to see through any defenses and assists in determining what direction to travel. During this important piece of the therapy, Carol can fall in love with the individual, uniting attention and unconditional love so that healing will occur.

What was resonating deep inside as I listened intently was the connection to one's spirit, which is the cornerstone of my journey to heal from cancer.

I gained a deeper insight into this mystical world as Carol imparted how shamanic work is restoring energy and spirit balance. Its magical soul retrieval is where the returning pieces of one's soul, light, and energy from which we lost access is aspired. The removal from an individual's body field of any energy that is not used, doesn't belong or serve one is accomplished.

It could be a simple belief picked up like, "I will not be loved." Carol then focuses on a healing release of that belief. With the belief, liberated, healthy love comes into one's life.

At the close of our conversation, Carol and I set a date for my session.

On a clear, crisp early spring morning, I traveled to Pownal, Vermont, to connect with Carol. Following her directions, I ended up on one of the many dirt roads found in the state of Vermont. I carefully navigated my way through woods harboring remnants of winter snow residing on the road's boundaries and clinging to trees on either side. Even here in the dense woods, spring was encroaching, for numerous patches of bare earth were eagerly waiting for the warmth of a new season to begin another cycle of growth. The sun's rays danced through the silent trunks of the trees that soon would sprout with life.

I continued my drive through the quietness, passing the few dwellings well hidden among the trees. My car followed the road's curve, and I came upon a clearing where Carol's home sat. I parked my Volkswagen in her driveway and was immediately greeted by two burly bundles of hair barking their welcome. Carol opened her front door and exclaimed that I had met her welcoming committee.

There was an instant bond with this gentle, smiling woman. Her bright personality embraced my being and tenderly eased my spirit into a space of comfort. She led me to the living room, where large windows invited the sun and nature in to stay. The glass passages to the outside world revealed the breathtaking view of the hills, valleys, and mountains of southwestern Vermont.

I settled into the sofa and took it all in. It is the perfect setting for a healer.

Carol offered tea in her sun-filled kitchen. We sat at the small, round table, conversing freely and openly for about thirty minutes. With a mug of warm tea in hand to fend off the chill of a March day, the conversation poured out words, memories, visuals, events, and people from my childhood, struggles with being gay, relationships, the cancer, and more. It was as if I was spending time catching up with an old friend.

From the exchange, Carol was able to set a direction for the session. She reviewed the format, and then we relocated to her healing space, located in one of the spare rooms.

Once in the room, I became aware of several crystals lining the floor beside the walls and covering shelves. Carol had me select one to possess while participating in the therapy. I chose the sparkling white-shaded quartz that caught my eye. I drew in its essence and went to lie down on the padded table. A warm blanket was positioned over me, and Carol began to thoughtfully select crystals of various sizes, shapes, and brilliance, placing them alongside and on top of my body. I felt secure and safe.

I relaxed, closed my eyes, and sank deeper into the table.

The drumming began. Carol chanted and drummed while moving around the table. At times, the drum was positioned directly over my body, moving up and down the entire length of my torso. I was in a trance and became one with the melodic rhythm, the chant's earthiness, and the instrument's movement. The vibrations penetrated my outer walls, allowing its hypnotic pulses to find their way to my core, cells, organs, and soul.

After a few minutes, the drumming and chanting ceased, and quiet began to reclaim the room. But before a silence could overtake the space, Carol's calming voice pierced the momentary stillness, issuing instructions to picture a favorite place or area. My mind wandered, yet I was careful not to force just any visual to appear automatically. I let it find me.

To my surprise, the visual that emerged was the field directly behind our farmhouse. I was puzzled at first as to why this image appeared, but an immediate awareness retrieved the reason. I have been spending a lot of time playing with the dogs in this meadow.

It is the hayfield, where its grasses are flattened by the winter winds and snow, where Polar and Macy and I enjoy our daily romp with nature.

I relish the freedom of its open space, where no walls hold me in, where there are no questioning students or adults, just the three of us inhaling the wide expanse framed by trees and hills.

It is where I let go of the day's confinement inside the school building and the car, and where Polar and Macy shake off the day's stiffness from being shut inside the house.

Out in the freedom of nature, the three of us explore and play. I take in the peace, while Polar and Macy frantically sniff the smells of the wildlife that visited our fields. As Macy explored, Polar, who has trained me to throw the ball, is able to release the pent-up energy trapped inside his Lab physique by chasing the round flying object. His simple pleasure in retrieving this prize so we can do it all again is endless.

This magical space bestows a wonderful and relaxing essence for spending early evenings playing with the dogs, embracing the stillness, and witnessing the spectacular colors of the setting sun as it gradually disappears behind the bare hills. It has become my sanctuary from the stresses of daily life.

I now understood why this place presented itself for today's healing journey.

I shared my visual with Carol, and she asked who was with me. I responded immediately, "Our dogs, Polar and Macy." Carol was delighted, and the journey began with Polar taking the lead as his sister, Macy, went off to explore on her own.

Polar guided me through the open expanse, connecting with the different events discussed earlier in the kitchen. One by one, they appeared and drew me into their realm. At one moment, I was a little boy, four or five years old, confused by the intrusion of various sentiments silently received from my parents and not understanding these emotional tokens or knowing what to do with them.

Carol gently escorted me in letting them go by, releasing each one into the wide-open field. I watched them float away. As the distance grew between us, a sense of lightness enveloped my entire body.

Next I was eleven years old, struggling, fighting, and terrified with the feelings I possessed of being different. I was different from the children around me, ashamed, racked with guilt for the distorted self-view. It was the beginning of my acknowledgment and struggle with being gay.

Polar then led me to my mom. A conversation on my parents' divorce and if it hinged on my being gay was being held. Her response was of a need, a desire to be happy.

I followed Polar as he ran to another part of the field, and suddenly a visual of embracing my dad came into focus—an image so powerful, so poignant, my voice cracked as I related the vision to Carol. She patiently stayed in the moment, sensing there would be more. There was. A picture exploded in front of me, its brilliance of light comforting as I observed myself, my dad, and Tim embracing. Polar danced around us, barking with pure joy.

I was overcome with emotions and needed to pause and let it ride out.

With the culmination of each event, Carol's reassurance of the lack of my role in its occurrence or consequences brought forth an awareness of peace, happiness, and oneness. Revisiting times of my youth, my twenties, forties, and fifties were freeing. I was able to obtain a new perspective in each important event and time.

As we approached the end of our healing travels, Carol asked, "Where is Polar now?"

My mind refocused on this animal gift, and I saw him near a stream on our property. I began to share this with Carol, when in mid-sentence I announced, "He's running now. He's running up to the house."

Pausing momentarily before responding I heard Carol's voice filled with a surprise question: "Polar is running toward the house?"

"Yes," I answered.

"Hmm, I wonder why. I thought he would be heading back to the field where we began," she responded.

At that moment, the door to the room was pushed open as one of Carol's dogs entered.

He approached the padded table, moving about, sniffing, and greeting. I was amused by the interruption and smiled at the added element to my journey. I had a feeling that something unexpected would emerge from the visit.

Carol, watching her dog, asked if it would be all right if he remained for a minute or two. I agreed, as his entrance was magical and his guidance desired. I closed my eyes and heard Carol's voice state, "Okay, I get it. Thank you." She excused herself to let the dog out and upon returning, took the new direction in stride, adding, "Let's see why Polar took us here."

We began a visual exploration of the house, with Carol asking about certain rooms. In each space, Carol revealed feelings or sensations acquired. The exploring continued until we reached one of the rooms downstairs.

Carol abruptly stopped and questioned the use of the space. Her explanation was that the room's aura and emotional essence was troubling.

Through gentle inquiries, details of a difficult situation I was presently confronting spilled out. As I shared, Carol connected the various elements of the circumstance, explaining what she sensed and received from the disclosure.

I listened intently, realizing how on-the-mark Carol's connections were; I was amazed and intrigued with the unfolding of this path, yet relieved with its presence. Carol relayed reasons why it was occurring, what would most likely transpire, and how I needed to be careful and not take on the toxic emotions of the dilemma. She delved deeper, mystically, and personally identifying the many components in this state of affairs. Her insights, concerns, and suggestions were a gift.

The emergence of this path was not planned, but I was grateful, as it was continually draining my energy and spirit. It was not a positive aura for healing.

Carol gave thanks and praise to Polar for leading us back to the house, so I could face the situation. I too rejoiced for this gentle, cherished animal and the acuity afforded in looking at the delicate and exhausting difficulty.

With the completion of my time in Carol's healing space, we sat once again at the kitchen table, reviewing the discoveries of the therapy.

It was and still is a very magical, perceptive, and healing voyage.

We parted, and I walked lightly to my car. As I exited the driveway, the sun caressed my face, encouraging a smile to grow. A calming sensation of peace, understanding, and healing embodied my whole being. I was cognizant that there would be more hurdles and demanding predicaments ahead, but now I possessed a deeper insight and knowledge on how to deal with each one.

I was filled with contentment as the car headed home to Greenwich, where I planned to give Polar and Macy a big hug.

Later that day, as the sun was slowly setting behind the hills, I played ball with Polar and watched Macy explore the field. A gigantic smile erupted, a smile embracing the beautiful gifts received earlier from Polar, Macy, and Carol.

Gratefulness soared through my veins, evoking a wonderful healing essence. I continued to smile as I gazed at all that was around me.

Just one more throw, Polar.

A Time of Reflection

The well is within us, and if we dig deeply in the present moment, the water will spring forth.

Thich Nhat Hanh

The 2011–2012 school year brought numerous challenges and surprises. Many new doors were opened, some closed, and many changes in my life were to occur. As I began my thirty-fourth year of teaching, I was unaware of the new paths that were to unfold. The late summer and early fall of 2011 incorporated back-to-school, the commute, an expanding need of energy for teaching, the beginning of the Buddhist study group, and my psychic experience with Tracy.

In September, I was refreshed and feeling more centered than I had in quite some time. The past year was consumed with the discovery of the second occurrence of breast cancer; the drug voyage; a demanding group of students; new avenues of healing with Maud, Bridgette, and John; a new oncologist; the addition of Dr. Lasneski; and the right mastectomy.

I was definitely ready for a better year.

With the school year progressing and my Buddhist study group blossoming and taking root, things were looking up. As months passed, I began to notice a familiar stirring of something amiss deep inside, especially at work. It was as though a part of me was missing in action. I was learning through the study group to be with the feeling, so I was with it.

I was with the sensation, and noticed I felt "off" emotionally in connecting with my teaching. I enjoyed the new group of students, yet something was not in place.

Another piece of my journey's puzzle was coming to light. Unable to secure the reason for its appearance, I associated this disconnect with the several draining events of the previous year. I kept tagging it to last year's difficult class, the cancer surgery, the drug war, and the mastectomy. "Why wouldn't I feel off? That would take a lot out of anyone," I reassured myself repeatedly.

Then I recognized I was living for the weekends, holidays, and school vacations. This was troubling, as I have always loved teaching. "What is going on?" became my question of the day.

Onward I plowed, hoping that some miracle would appear, and my old self would resurface. I connected for the first time that fall with Tracy, and it helped to calm the stirring for a while. But eventually, the inner emotional whirlwind let its presence be known. Each time I sensed the altercation within, I would once again ascribe it to the prior year's happenings.

In all honesty, the struggle was extremely disconcerting since teaching was a passion for over thirty years of my life. I continued to sit with the feeling.

Or was I really sitting *on* it, wanting to squash or hide it from view? I needed to open my heart and trust the answer would be provided when the time was right.

I opened to the fear—well, at least partially. I plodded on, listening to my heart, but unbeknownst to me, fear was masterly gaining the upper hand.

Outside of school, I was busy with family and friends, reading, working on the house, and studying the Buddhist philosophy. I believed all was well in each facet of my life. Colleagues, friends, and family remarked on how healthy I looked. I embraced the comforting observations, but a feeling of emptiness, of personal misplacement was maturing.

In time, I came to the realization my heart was not fully present in my teaching, and it was slowly taking an enormous toll on my students and me.

Neither they nor I were able to uncover, to see and enjoy the true me, the true Mr. K.

It was an unsettling revelation. Although my conclusion for this recognition still harbored the depleting circumstances of the preceding year, I suspected deep down there was more to it than just last year's occurrences. I felt defeated, for teaching was who I was.

Throughout the ongoing struggle, the image of a hot-air balloon frequently popped up in my mind. As the balloon graced the sky, offering the wide-open view of the world from its vantage point high in the atmosphere, somewhere in this majestic object, a tear so small, so tiny allowed its precious air to escape slowly. With the constant release of the needed ether, its vital spirit, the fragile balloon gradually descended to the ground.

This was me. My spirit was diminishing, vanishing right before my eyes. I was steadily deflating.

I sat with Tim and shared my struggle and thoughts. From our discussion, the decision to complete this year and the following school year was made. For a short time following this momentous conclusion, I felt grounded and trudged forward. But soon the emptiness and struggle to be at school returned. Only now it was much stronger and more intense.

I was confused, frustrated, and unable to put my finger on the pulse of this challenge.

Yet the journey continued with my doctors, healers, insights through readings, reflecting, meditating, and focused on being in the present. Each of these positive behaviors helped me cope, but was I truly living? Even with the decision to retire from teaching in 2013, my heart was heavy, my head cloudy, my energy and spirit retreating, and a personal situation with a friend was taking a substantial toll on my psyche.

Something had to change. I knew and believed the answer was within. I thought the solution was found and the tear in my balloon repaired, but I uncovered that I had only barely patched the tiny hole, and it was leaking once more.

This plight was far more critical, for I discovered it was a much larger opening that required additional compassionate attention.

My mind-set was of being in the present, open, and trusting that a resolution to this quandary would reveal itself.

Once again, the universe came knocking, and the well within me was able to supply the courage and insight to make the needed change.

Knock, Knock, It's the Universe Calling

Usually we're so caught up in ourselves, we're hanging on to ourselves so tightly, it takes a Mack truck knocking us down, to wake us up, and stop our minds.

Pema Chodron

At the beginning of March, a couple of events transpired that, when pieced together, brought forth a significant decision.

On the first Friday in March, a teacher meeting was held in my building. I was unable to attend, because a friend and colleague, Deb, needed to talk. While the forum took place down the hall from my classroom, Deb and I discussed a struggle she was currently experiencing.

What I wasn't aware of was how the teacher meeting's topic would provide another piece of the puzzle in my present struggle.

As Deb and I concluded our talk, people streamed out of the meeting. I approached one of the teachers walking by and asked about the gathering. She replied that it centered on an agreement (to be voted on) between the teacher association and the district for a pay freeze next year. I was stunned.

Well aware of the financial difficulties confronting many school districts, my initial reaction to this news was anger. Anger based on the fact that the district had provided a generous retirement incentive for administrators the previous year. Many left with wonderful advantages, and here I was looking at leaving next year and dealing with a pay freeze. My head was heavier and my mind cloudier with this news.

The following Monday, I met with my financial advisor, Whit Merrill. We got together in my classroom after the students' dismissal. I enjoy meeting with Whit, because his easy personality created a comfortable environment in which to discuss money. He had contacted me weeks earlier about meeting and reviewing my personal-retirement portfolio. Whit went over his insights on what he felt we should focus on. Before he could continue, I informed Whit of my intention to retire next year.

His response, "Why not this year?" took me completely by surprise. My whole being recoiled as if struck by a powerful object, which in this case was a compelling thought.

I reeled back and automatically blurted out, "Well, I've got to save money. We have barns to fix and things in the house to update." The words were spluttering out as quickly as my mind created them.

Whit looked at me and shared, "Michael, you can dip into your 403 plan at fifty-five if you are retired." I sat still, dazed, slowly digesting the information.

I was taken aback as my inner voice took over and asked, *Now why would my financial advisor make such a statement?* I nodded to acknowledge the thought gifted by Whit and sensed it was finding a home within.

Our meeting came to a close, so I gathered my things and started the commute home. During the trip, this thought, this crazy idea was gently tucked away deep inside, allowing it to simmer and evolve.

Wednesday was a trying day at school; my level of patience was low, and I struggled to understand why. Its reason emerged as I constructed substitute plans for the following day. The reason was fear.

As I completed the plans for the substitute teacher, I recognized the presence of fear for the upcoming chest MRI being done tomorrow in Bennington. This test came about from sharing with my oncologist the comment by Dr. Lasneski, the homeopathic physician, that he sensed "cells" in my left chest area. The observation raised my concern level. Even with using the tools of meditation, the breath, and positive thoughts, I was troubled by the statement.

Dr. Ives's response was, "Okay, let's have a look, Michael. I'll set up an MRI." I felt relieved yet an old familiar concern was bubbling within. So here I was late Wednesday afternoon, writing up teaching plans and acknowledging the fear.

That evening, I shared my discovery with Tim. In the midst of uncovering the realization for him, I heard my voice reveal, "I am finding how scared I still am that the cancer may return. I see how anxious and agitated I become prior to a doctor visit or a medical test. I don't want to live in fear. I don't want to be scared. I don't want to give more power to this disease."

The words erupted from my soul and punctured the air around me. I thought I had overcome the fear of another occurrence. I definitely needed to sit with this.

With all the work I have been doing—the meditation, healers, doctors, nutrition, and readings—the blasted fear was still able to show its face.

It is amazing how old habits and thoughts keep resurfacing. In my journey, I have discovered they return as lessons, reminders that we are running low, running on an emotional emptiness. They seize any opportunity to re-emerge and take our spiritual bank hostage.

Fear, its power and toxic tentacles, patiently wait until one's attention, one's empowerment is low.

I had to rescue my emotional base. I recognized the return of fear, and that was the first step.

The MRI was done, and Friday I was back at school, running on autopilot. The heaviness and fog in my head was intensifying. Luckily, on Saturday I had an appointment with John. I cherish the energy sessions with John, for it is where I reclaim a sense of centeredness.

Saturday morning, I robotically drove to Pownal, Vermont. Heaviness of heart and a head filled with a foggy distraction were my companions as I traveled the familiar roads. Throughout the drive, I was immersed in a self-conversation, oblivious to the surrounding scenery.

My head felt distant as thoughts pounded, their rhythm striking like the sound of a lonely buoy's bell ringing in the open water, the melodic beat in concert with the waves. The solitary bell's chimes announced its location, but its presence was masked by a heavy fog.

I was in a personal haze. The exhaustion was evident, for its effects were both physical and emotional. As I approached John's home, the scent of the burning wood fueling his woodstove extended an invitation to its warmth and the safety within.

I inhaled its essence, smiled, and entered the house. I was where I needed to be.

John welcomed me in, stepped back, and asked, "So, what were the results of the MRI?"

I wearily looked at him and replied, "I don't know yet. I'll know next week when I meet with Dr. Ives."

John, with a look of concern, offered, "Well, we can find out now."

I gazed at him somewhat startled out of surprise or fear and responded, "Won't that be stepping on someone's toes?"

John remarked, "That doesn't concern me now. If you are nervous about the results, we should get them."

The words that followed, that stumbled out of me like a rockslide expelling itself from my mind, shook my being to its core.

I stood by his front door and told him, "It's okay. I'll wait. You know, John, if they find cancer cells, I'll just retire this year."

The words just released amassed into an ominous cloud surrounding my entire being. Immediately I recognized the venom that had gained freedom. Stunned and shocked at what I had just uttered, John and I looked at each other, the silence between us so telling.

John was the first to speak and gently pointed out the obvious. "Michael, do you realize what you just said?" Still numbed and shocked, I stood rigid, barely able to nod in recognition of his question. He went on to say, "Michael, you are inviting the cancer to come back, to make your decision for you." I nodded in silent agreement, for I held the very same conclusion.

Finally, after a few quiet moments, I managed to set free the words, "I know." As they crossed my lips and entered the verbal and conscious reality, tears congregated around my eyes. They slowly gathered and then one by one trickled down my face.

I released a sigh that traveled from an inner depth, a place where truth is held prisoner.

A soft-toned whisper tinged with strength set free an emotional truth: "I don't want to go back there next year, John." With its liberation from deep inside, my body relaxed. The expulsion of a truth held prisoner gave way to peace.

John's sympathetic voice emerged out of the haunting cloud, the fog surrounding me. "You know, Michael, the last time you were here, you stated how your heart wasn't in your teaching, yet you were planning to go back next year. After you left, I kept wondering why."

I looked at this insightful man who was able to see deep within me and with total honesty shared, "Fear, John, fear. We have the mortgage and other expenses that would be difficult on a reduced retirement."

By granting fear its freedom, I felt it floating away. *Expenses or health?* my inner voice questioned with love. I smiled because I knew the answer was *health*.

In that moment, I knew to trust and follow my heart, to trust my inner voice, the inner wisdom.

To trust, yes trust the universe.

John and I sat with the momentous revelation. As I shared with him the events of the past eight days, I was able to interconnect each incident's role to this moment, this conclusion, this decision. The freezing of the salaries, Whit's comments, the struggle at school, the MRI insight, and today's disclosure—all these pieces when fused together conferred the message of "Move on and live!"

That evening, I relayed the day's discovery to Tim, with its message to retire this year. The heavy baggage I had clung to and carried evaporated.

On Monday, after firing up the classroom's computer, I constructed the letter of intent to retire. I was free. I also received great news from Dr. Ives that the MRI was clear. The fog was lifting and dissipating into the vast space.

Now a distinct, clear vision the ocean buoy was slightly rocking on gentle waves chiming its presence for all to see.

It sat on calm water, covered by bright-blue skies for miles on end.

Tattoo Becoming Whole: Physically and Emotionally

We are our most whole when we are healing ourselves.

Michael Meade

In late winter, Tim and I were in Albany, on our way to my general practitioner's office for the yearly physical. I was in the midst of an inner tempestuous roller coaster. As we traveled, my head was consumed with the events of my struggle, for it would be a few weeks down the road before the decision to retire was made. On Washington Avenue, we passed the Plastic Surgery Group's office building. I pointed it out to Tim, recalling the nipple reconstruction back in 2007. The images of the surgery and the trip to New Jersey where the new nipple was tattooed settled in my mind. I was now nipple-free from the cancer surgery and mastectomy.

Traveling onward to Dr. Kelleher's office, the word *tattoo* kept echoing in my head. But why?

As the word swirled around inside my mind, it suddenly dawned on me that Diane, the tattoo artist, comes to the Plastic Surgery Group's office each spring and fall.

Listening to the inner voice of wisdom, I turned the car around and headed back to the brick office building, telling Tim my idea. As I entered the large waiting room, memories flooded back.

This makes so much sense, I confidently expressed to myself as I waited to speak to the receptionist. After explaining my situation and history with Dr. Rockmore, the receptionist at the front desk contacted his office. Within a few minutes, Nancy from Dr. Rockmore's office came out to the waiting room to speak with me. She graciously listened and relayed that Diane was expected in the early spring.

Thank you, universe!

She took the needed information and said that they would be in contact to set up a date and time for the tattooing.

I left the building, stood for a moment, took in a deep breath, and smiled. My inner voice and heart had spoken, and I trusted them without delay. Silently I thanked the universe again for unfolding this occurrence.

Back in the car, I shared with Tim what had transpired. He gave a smile of love and support.

Since the mastectomy in June, I had grown accustomed to the scars and absent nipples on my chest. Reconstruction was not considered, because in the deepest depths of my heart and core, I was done with surgery. I wanted no more intrusions or invasions in my body.

Yet something was amiss. An incompleteness that had been overshadowed by the present emotional turmoil was granted its freedom simply by a glimpse of the Plastic Surgery Group's building. The memories released uncovered a hidden yearning for completion, for some sort of normalcy, for healing. I believed this path with the tattoos would help me feel whole.

Now, don't get me wrong, I am eternally grateful for my physical and emotional health with this illness, but I must admit feeling different, incomplete with having a chest lacking nipples. They were a part of me until the cancer.

The unearthing of this discovery struck a chord within, for I had been holding the belief in an emotional and physical contentment following the mastectomy. Yet, the gratification held no longer seemed to be enough.

But I have learned, traveling this remarkable voyage, that the universe knows and guides us to where we need to be. Our role is to listen and trust.

Within a few weeks, I received the call setting a date and time for the tattooing. By this time, I had made the decision to retire and was in a peaceful space that only heightened my level of joy.

The day of the appointment, I entered the waiting room filled with awe and anticipation. Soon, I was following Diane to the examining room where she had set up shop. Sitting in one of the chairs, I immediately shared how she had tattooed my reconstructed nipple back in January 2008. But I added that the nipple was lost to the second cancer surgery and the right one to a mastectomy.

Diane listened and sensed my yearning for normalcy. She gently explained what would occur; I stood up and was ready to begin. We spent time discussing the location of the tattoos; then, confident that I was fine with their placement, Diane began to create.

While she tattooed, we talked and shared on a variety of topics. Before I knew it, Diane was giving me instructions on the necessary care for the new tattoos. Within an hour of entering this room of artistic creation, I left the proud owner of two tattooed nipples. It brought me back to January 2008, standing on the shore, breathing in the wonder of coming full circle that year, and a sense of completion and wholeness.

Four years later I was welcoming a deeper sense of gratitude. Now, when I look in a mirror, the tattooed nipples gift the deep-rooted belief of being whole.

For many of us who have journeyed with breast cancer, tattooing is the last step in a passage to heal and feel complete. It provides a sense of wholeness in the physical realm, in concert with a deep penetration in one's emotional well.

My well has filled to a capacity and recognition of a fullness not detected since the cancer's discovery in 2007.

The tattooed nipples have bestowed a sense of peace and are an integral part of a deeper physical, emotional, and spiritual awakening. Their presence has caressed back to life a piece of me hidden deep inside that is now beginning to heal.

As I began to write this book, I had an opportunity to speak with Diane about her work. I had been curious as to how this woman from New Jersey ended up connecting with the Plastic Surgery Group in Albany, New York. In February 2013, I contacted Diane, and in our conversation, she shared the story.

Diane Lange and her husband, Steve, own Moonlight Tattoo in Seaville, New Jersey. About twenty years ago, Diane was at a tattoo convention in Schenectady, New York. There she came across Dr. Lynch, one of the original founders of the Plastic Surgery Group. He was at the convention, seeking a female tattoo artist who could work on his patients.

Back then, physicians like Dr. Lynch had tattooing kits but were not experts at providing the needed level of artistry. Dr. Lynch wanted someone for the women who had endured breast cancer and its accompanying surgeries.

After observing Diane's work at the convention, he invited her to come up to Albany. Intrigued by this path, Diane was reluctant at first, since she had never worked on this type of client. She decided to jump in and try it. Surprisingly, Diane discovered this type of service was not as available as one might think.

The women who come to see Diane are very different from her regular clients, in that many, if not all, are crippled emotionally for not being who or what they were. These women are very receptive to what Diane is providing and treat her like gold.

Over time, with much adjusting, she was able to perfect how to get the tattoo on women, eventually utilizing pigments used for portraits. As we conversed, Diane hit on an area close to my heart: the meaning of this healing act.

In spending time with so many women, Diane has recognized and respects that time with her represents the end. It is the final, magical step in what is a long and painful journey with the disease. The women take it very strongly.

For Diane, it is slightly different, because she deals with body parts all the time. I know for me, the sessions with Diane induced a sense of wholeness and completion.

It is a subtle realization, not having a nipple or in my case, nipples, but it is there. It was present each time I looked at my chest.

Providing this wonderful gift to so many, Diane has been endowed with being grounded. It is a wake-up call each spring and fall as to what is important.

Diane has shared her creative healing for more than twenty years in the Albany area, having tattooed more than five hundred women and three men.

My gratitude to the universe for the crossing of paths with this exceptional, artistic individual knows no bounds.

Insight to a New Direction

*Create a new version of who you would
become, and you surely will become it.*

Dan Millman

As the close of the school year was approaching, I was both elated and terrified. I had been a teacher for thirty-four years and was now wondering who I would be as this career came to its end. Being a teacher had always defined who I was.

I noticed a quiet inner struggle, and learning from the past, I let it be, trusting it would reveal itself when ready. Colleagues began inquiring what my plans in retirement were, and I shared a verbal map of a post-teaching career.

When school was done, Tim and I were driving out to Provo, Utah, for my nephew Kyle's wedding. On the way out to Utah and back to New York, we would visit some of the national parks. Once home, I would help a friend with his goat-cheese operation and in late fall substitute teach.

I had to admit that subbing was not high on my agenda, but it was a known and safe route. Interestingly, I began adding to the list a feeling that there was something else, but it hadn't presented itself yet.

There was a stirring slowly coming to the forefront, and I just needed to be patient.

The last few weeks of school were filled with many wonderful gifts. Former students, parents, and colleagues came to say good-bye and shared special moments and thanks. I was leaving on a high note and trusted the process of life would unfold the next path.

At the end of a Reiki session in June, Maud asked if I would be open and comfortable seeing her friend Mary, who is a counselor. With the sensing of a blockage around my heart, Maud believed it would be beneficial to talk with Mary about letting go of teaching.

Letting go of teaching— of course, this was the base of my struggle. The letting go of my identity of thirty-four years. As the realization hit home, I shared about the heaviness and agreed the idea of talking to Mary was a good one.

It is still astounding how certain souls cross my path, encouraging and guiding me to explore new avenues. It was to happen once again.

I drove to Mary's office on a sunny Wednesday morning. The sky was clear, and the sun caressed my face as I traveled to Cambridge, New York. Mary's office was located in an old brick building on Main Street in the village. I climbed the wooden stairs to the second floor, where a waiting room ushered its welcome. Mary came out, extended a warm greeting, and led me to her office, which was filled with comfortable furniture and décor.

I sank into an oversized chair, felt at ease, and began to share the details of my healing journey, retirement, the trip out west, working with goats and cheese, and substitute teaching. While I was vibrantly sharing my passage, Mary sat smiling, taking in each gesture and emotion put forth. When I was finished, Mary kindly and gently interjected, "Michael, I hope you won't get too involved with the subbing."

I gazed at her, wondering if unenthusiastic vibes about substitute teaching were picked up. Asking why, I anxiously waited to hear her reply. Mary smiled and simply stated, "Because I see a book here."

My body retracted into the comfortable embrace of the chair as I added, "You know, Mary, you are not the first person to say that to me." I sat still for a moment, allowing the telling events and images to surface. Each incident pieced together constructed another section of my healing journey's puzzle. Together they unveiled a new path, a true path.

I expounded on each revealing occurrence, conversation, and action where the concept of writing was offered. Mary sat back and took in my words.

"First, I remember shortly after receiving the second diagnosis, a colleague at school approached me. Donna, who was dealing with breast cancer and enduring radiation and chemotherapy, came up and hugged me compassionately. In the midst of the embrace,

Donna whispered, 'Michael, I feel it is back because you need to go out and teach people about this.'

"I thanked her, and the words presented, this idea was gently tucked away inside. My yoga teacher, colleagues, and friends have periodically stated that I need to write about my journey and how I am choosing to heal. Again, these wonderful expressions were not dismissed, but allowed to find a home within. And just recently, my friend Tish down in Virginia remarked about my retiring, 'Michael, I feel you are done with teaching in the public schools, but you are not done with teaching.' Then there is your insight, Mary.

"Somehow, my spirit knew that these precious words possessed a special meaning and would become known at the right time. I am sensing that right now, this moment, is that time."

Mary smiled and nodded at the messages of guidance that had flowed to me and were being embraced. I glanced at this perceptive individual who guided me to uncover a new, emerging path being born as I closed doors to the old, giving room for the new.

Without thought as to what I was going to share, the words just magically poured out. "You know, I've always wanted to write. It has been a deep secret and dream for so long." Mary's face said it all.

Our session ended, and I walked away knowing to let today's discovery take root, percolate, be nurtured, and become part of me. I headed home with a smile that covered my face and wondered, "Am I a writer and teacher of this journey?" I let the words settle and find a home, recognizing they were safe and present.

The gift was unveiling its contents. I was ready for the trip out west and ready to explore the next chapter in my journey.

Thank you, universe!

Westward Bound

Notice the blue sky, the child's smile, the beautiful sunrise.

Thich Nhat Hanh

With the car packed and my fifteen-year-old nephew James part of the crew, we set off. We would visit a few national parks on our way to Utah and others while traveling back to New York.

Leaving the daily routines gave precious time to think and reflect. My public school teaching career had drawn to its close, and a new, adventurous path was beginning to unfold. The trip out west was its starting point.

So much had happened these past five years: the discovery of breast cancer in 2007 and 2010, surgeries, struggles, the drug dilemma, healers and doctors, and momentous life changes.

I strongly sensed and understood the importance of this expedition.

There is a wonderful restorative power in the beauty of nature. In the coming weeks, I would be exposed to places, events, and souls, each igniting a deeper spiritual and emotional healing.

It began with embracing the simple pleasures in each day.

The Gifts Unwrapped

Every time we get back in touch with ourselves, the conditions become favorable for us to encounter life in the present moment.

Thich Nhat Hanh

A few days, into the journey, I felt grounded again. So many events, decisions, and healings occurred during the past five years as I was imprisoned with a daily routine of survival. The commute, teaching, numerous doctor visits, personal dramas, and a healing education were physically and emotionally draining.

This trip, with its freedom, enabled me to plug the hole, which was allowing my energy and spirit to escape. Every moment was in the now, the present. Each day on the road brought new sights, an endless sky, the warmth of the sun, breathtaking countryside, the natural medicine my spirit was craving.

Being present yielded an ability to deal with worries or concerns right there. It was a daily lesson. When a concern like my future financial fate, a new job, or the idea of substitute teaching arose, I would close my eyes (if I was not driving at the time) and release the phrase, "At this moment, I am fine, and all is well." It created a space of enjoying where I was and who I was with. I chose to not empower the thoughts and to live in the moment. With this behavior, I enjoyed the expanse of Lake Erie, the colors of summer, the people, and the beauty of the land.

The concerns and worries were there, relegated to the back seat, and the established presence of a trust in the process of life to help me sort them out in the right time and place. Now was for taking in all that was before me.

One of the many gifts from our adventure out west was the time spent in Provo with my sister Janet and her family. They had moved out to Utah more than twenty years ago. Since I do not enjoy traveling by plane, our time together has been sporadic over the years. The visit to Provo was an occasion to connect and re-establish old bonds.

With all of us gathered in Utah for the wedding, it was a family reunion. Accompanying Tim and me from New York were my mom and my brother's family. Connecting, sharing, and cherishing each other was the theme of our stay.

On Sunday evening, a few of us sat outside on my sister's patio, talking and visiting. Gathered around the table, we shared stories and laughs. My eyes kept tearing as I looked around at those seated beside me and felt a warmth pulse throughout my being. I knew it was from a healing originating from the love present.

It was a gentle nudge from the universe to take in the essence of this moment, this time, this family. I was embracing the healing energy received from those around me and was full of gratitude for family.

Over the years, my definition of family evolved. There is the one you are born into, the one you marry or partner into, and the one comprised of the special souls you treasure traveling your life path.

During the time I was in the midst of the struggle with an acceptance of being gay, a self-induced distance from my family grew. The people I came to know through work, friendships, and social connections became family. They, along with my birth family, are an integral facet in my ability to heal. Included in my definition of family are the animals that grace our lives each day. I know firsthand the unconditional love and support these gentle creatures grant us humans.

However, a family group is a source of healing, one very simple and true.

The next day, Tim and I set off to visit Grand Teton National Park and Yellowstone. My nephew James was staying in Provo to hang out with family. I was immersed in the natural wonder and healing potential of each special place.

It was here that I let go. I realized how often the crowded routines and rushing about of daily life had blinded me to the graceful spirit of nature. Once I was physically removed from the day-to-day conditions, my senses began to sharpen and open to the spirit and wonder of our world. I consciously observed the beautiful sky, the diverse landscapes soothing my soul, and a spiritual connection to the beings honoring us with their presence on this planet. All were healing essences I inhaled deeply to keep within.

Being able to encounter the natural world while witnessing the awe of humans experiencing its wonders gave birth to a deeper mystical healing.

It was these enlightened moments that strengthened a belief that it is not just doctors, drugs, supplements, our thoughts, and beliefs that assist us to heal, but the magical power of our environment. To observe the gracefulness of a deer, the erratic path of a rabbit, the stillness of a flower, the wet nose of a dog, a cat's soft purr, and the tender touch of a friend or loved one can bring an inner restorative peace. It is the spirit of each simple act that penetrates your core and uncovers the healing soul we yearn and search for. We just need to be in touch with ourselves and in the present moment to welcome this life force in.

A metaphysical consciousness would come to a healing fruition as I became one with the spirit of the Grand Canyon.

On our way to the Grand Canyon, Tim, James, and I had spent time at Zion and Bryce National Parks. We explored and connected with the serene beauty and earthiness of each unique setting.

While driving to the Canyon's North Rim, I detected an inner sense this sacred site's draw and peacefulness would be magical.

We arrived early Friday evening and decided to explore near the lodge before driving back to our accommodations outside the park's boundaries. The three of us walked along the paths, taking us to different vistas of this sacred space. A lifelong fear of heights held me back from investigating areas where Tim and James ventured. While they easily climbed the rock formations and cliffs offering spectacular views, I took refuge on the path.

I walked paths where in places the rails were absent, instilling some uncomfortable reactions, especially where one can observe the depth of the drop down. From past experience, I relied on the true and trusted tool of looking down on the path as I proceeded onward.

When a rock grouping was present on one side of the passageway, I was able to walk with my eyes positioned straight ahead by simply placing my hand lightly on the rocks for a sense of security.

Eventually, I mustered the courage to climb and explore a small outcropping of rocks, which provided a breathtaking scene.

As the sun slowly set, the canyon's colors came alive in a variety of mystical shades. Sitting quietly and still, I took in the colorful landscape and let it find a home within. Dusk was taking hold, so we headed toward the lodge to check out the sights. With daylight fading and the absence of rails along the route, I fell back to walking with my eyes downward. Closer to the lodge were rocks I could touch, giving me the courage to look forward. I occasionally stopped to breathe in strength, but also to inhale the presence of this natural home.

I slowly pushed on with my hand on the rocks as we drew closer to our destination.

It was near the lodge where I came upon a woman sitting quietly on a rock. She was gazing out at the canyon. As I approached, she smiled and remarked, "You too?"

Understanding the greeting, an instant kinship for this fellow height-fearing soul materialized. I laughed out loud and replied, "Oh yeah." Tim continued walking to an observation deck that jutted out beyond the canyon's rim. Watching him move on, this gentle individual relayed that her friend was out there, but she had decided to stay put where safety called. We looked at each other and nodded in a silent acknowledgement of, "No way am I going out there!"

In our zone of comfort, we introduced ourselves. This graceful woman's name escapes me, but her warm smile is a wonderful memory. While we waited for our companions, we shared and conversed. They had traveled from her home in Springfield, Missouri, to visit some national parks. I shared details of our trip from upstate New York, my recent retirement, the journey with cancer, its role in this excursion out west, and the healing I'd already received from this voyage.

Her friend returned, and they were leaving to explore other areas. We said our good-byes, hugged, and before turning to move on, this kind soul bestowed a gift. She looked into my eyes, smiled, and put my hand in hers and passionately stated, "Just have a kick-ass life, Michael. Just have a kick-ass life!"

A laugh rang out as her words and their meaning embraced my inner being. I hugged this beautiful gift and replied, "I know in my heart and soul I was to connect with you right here, right now, and receive those words to live by."

With that said, this tender spirit departed, but her words are here with me, a part of me, and they nourish my spirit each day with each breath.

The next day, we drove to various lookout points bordering the North Rim. We discovered numerous locations, exposing a majestic panorama of the canyon. Throughout the day, we came across quiet settings where one can reflect and absorb the energy gifted by this wonder of nature.

In these special places, I would feel the sun's warm rays caress my whole body. Instinctively, I'd raise my arms out wide, close my eyes, and welcome in the magical, spiritual powers of the moment. In this meditative stance, the peace encountered was very real, very calm, very comforting.

As I stood still, my entire physique opened, and I sensed the gentle invasion of a warm glow rising up through my feet, which were securely rooted to the earth. It continued its restorative voyage up my legs, swirling vibrantly in my torso, enveloping my heart, and pausing momentarily in my head before exiting and cascading down my sides, lovingly encasing my being.

I was a welcome visitor, embraced by the many healing spirits residing in this magical abode. Never before had I detected or undergone such wondrous healing sensations.

We began our passage homeward to New York. The trip was periodically interrupted with a few stops along the way, and I was in deep reflection of the past three weeks. Of all the fascinating locations visited, the Northern Rim holds a special place. Its natural exquisite beauty, intense healing spirit, and the medicinal advice from my fellow traveler from Missouri are vital, eloquent forces in my journey to heal.

They are gifts, tools, and enlightened energy I utilize when in the midst of fear or uncertainty with the choices and risks of everyday life.

These are treasured awards from nature, my teacher and kindred spirit from Missouri, and of course, the universe.

A New Path Unfolds

Now is the time to put myself at the center of my life.

Meredith L. Young-Sowers

As summer blended into fall and the days inched their way to a new year, I kept in touch with my heart and inner voice. Challenges were met with meditation, compassion, and reflection. In the fall, retirement hit home, in that I was not returning to school but periodically helping my friend Jeff with his goats and cheesemaking. This new routine was freeing, and I was preparing to enter the world of substitute teaching.

Yet there was something present, a feeling, a desire, a dream tenderly asserting itself and quietly articulating a message of *wait ... wait ... there is something more, something different*. I listened to the whispers of my heart and soul and patiently waited.

The required completion date for the substitute-teaching application was fast approaching; still I waited. The observation of my uncertainty and hesitation was duly noted. Its gift: the unveiling of an inner sense, a need, to embark on a new route.

Subbing was safe, a known entity, comfortable, but the unknown passage was somewhat scary. With a reduced income, I recognized a focus on the material aspect rather than the emotional. Fear was determined to stay on a familiar course, but my reluctance in completing the application was a telling sign.

My soul was crying out, *Take a risk and face the fear*. In stillness, I was able to hear those words, and as I listened, I was led.

The new path being unveiled was an acknowledgement, a need, an inclination to write about my journey with breast cancer. There was a longing to share, in my own words and emotions, this voyage to investigate new horizons, take on risks, and follow a dream.

My heart was partnering with fate to discover my destiny. I needed to write.

Sitting down with Tim and discussing my intention not to substitute teach would reveal a powerful lesson that demanded to be embraced. It would confront the fear from my logical side that clamored for the security of an income from subbing and released the aspiration to follow my soul.

One evening, Tim asked if I had filled out the application. I sat down and joined him at the dining room table, stating how I was going to withdraw money out of my personal retirement account for the winter. His immediate response was that it wasn't a good idea, and the money should be saved for a rainy day.

Instantly, my old behavior surfaced, and anger took the lead. Inside, anger's voice rang out. *Save it for a rainy day? I've had cancer twice. Why would I save it for a rainy day?* Then, reverting to the tried-and-true old habit, I shut down and left the table to stew.

A few days later, in a conversation with Maud, I shared the interaction and my inability to say what I wished to impart. Maud, with her knack for seeing things clearly, gently shared, "Michael, when we approach situations where we are looking for approval, it rarely works out the way we would like it to."

The light bulb in my mind flashed, for this was an a-ha moment. I was taking in the whole picture. I smiled at Maud, who is not only a healer, but a trusted and treasured friend.

I must speak from my soul.

The next evening, I began a conversation with Tim on a different level. This time, my voice originated from my inner being. Sharing the desire to follow my heart, I reviewed how the past five years were tumultuous. With the cancer, surgeries, the drugs' effects, the job, the commute, and a draining situation with a friend, there was an inner need to forgo substitute teaching. Then, with a determination not seen before, I passionately stated how I yearned to put me first for once. A realization had taken hold of a desire to move on from this teaching career.

Tim listened as I vocalized how for fifty-six years, I have always put others' needs before mine. I knew its base was believing I was not good enough; it also centered on not loving myself. I desperately wanted, needed to claim my spirit back.

In my youth, it was family and friends who came first. As an educator, it was students, parents, and my school that took the lead spot. In adult life, it was work, family, and friends. Where was I? I was at the back of the line, pretending to be happy.

Yet, as intense as the past five years had been, they've been a valuable learning time. The cancer granted the liberation of the belief to love myself enough to secure the position at the head of the line.

"I need to write. I need to share in words and emotions all that I experienced. It is a gift I must give to myself."

Tim looked at me, smiled, and relayed that he understood the need to take this path.

I had spoken from the depths of my soul, releasing an inner truth.

Thanks, Maud.

The climactic shift was based on trust, a trust in its direction, and a trust in the process of life.

That November, I began the new path with the written word. My journey with breast cancer, a rarity in men, was ready to be shared. It was a route I had to do for myself and my healing.

For in following our heart and soul's message, we are willing to take a risk and uncover the truth of our dreams and our fate, and discover our true life path as it unfolds.

Awakened

Many drown in the commotion of life simply because they refuse to awaken to a dream they carry from birth.

Michael Meade

In pursuing the path of writing, I acknowledged a dream held for so long. Inside was a craving for creative expression. Interestingly, the dream began with an intention to write children's books.

As an elementary teacher, my favorite times of the school day were when we gathered on the rug for story time. The sharing of a tale, its magical words, and moments of being quiet and enjoying a book were enchanting. The joy received from reading aloud was immense. Thus, an aspiration for writing was born and came to fruition with this journey to awaken, to follow a dream, and to trust the process of the universe's direction and guidance.

For years before the move or even knowing of Washington County, I had visualized living in an old farmhouse, surrounded by fields. A gentle reminder of this visual was shared by my friends Christine and Diane, who were visiting one summer day. Before leaving to head home to Maine, Diane stated, "Michael, I'm so glad your visions came true." Confused by the statement, I asked her what she meant. Diane recalled the numerous conversations held in which I shared this vision over the years. I smiled, realizing the dream released so long ago had come true.

There was something magical, mystical at that instant, with the discovery that I was living a visualization I'd embraced for years. It was another a-ha moment tinged with a spiritual essence that was to grace me once more while writing.

During the daily writing sessions, I periodically would stop and gaze out the window near my desk. In these times of regrouping and stillness, I would take in the rural setting, observing the abandoned barns located across the road. Each structure within its walls holds wonderful stories from the past but now stands silent.

It was during one of these peaceful interludes that an old visual resurfaced, one in which I am at my desk, writing, taking a minute or two to be still while looking out the window. Although the vision originated from years past, it has played repeatedly in my mind like an old newsreel. And here in this present time, I was reflecting the exact behavior.

This realization brought an awakening to the power of visuals released to the universe and how they came to reality when I was ready to accept them. Thinking back to the first diagnosis, there were times when I would visualize myself as a healthy, vibrant individual who was no longer confined to cancer's boundaries. The vision unfolded once I became mindful of its ability to heal.

I hold a deep belief that visions are a powerful, positive medicine. As I envision where I may go or who I may be, it sets off a reaction inside. This inner retort encourages and promotes a healing at the cellular level, guiding my dreams to become a reality.

On my desk sits a plaque stating, *"If you can dream it, YOU CAN DO IT!"* This insightful phrase from Walt Disney says it all. They are words I repeat out loud, and each time, they unleash a stronger determination to take a risk, to face the fear, and to pursue my dream.

The process of writing has been a tremendous extension of my journey to heal. It is not a voyage presenting cancer as a wound or myself as a victim, but one of sharing the gifts received from such a dreaded illness. This disease, feared yet fought valiantly by many, had galvanized an inner desire to discover my true self and true life dream. As Michael Meade states in his book, *Fate and Destiny: The Two Agreements of the Soul*, "Being fully awake means to become able to see and follow the dream of one's life, wherever it might lead."

I had become conscious of my dream by traveling this journey.

The excursion with this personal composition imparted a spectator's view of my struggles and triumphs with cancer. The disease was a catalyst for not only uncovering the strength and courage to confront the illness, but to muster the same qualities and confront my inner self.

It presented an opportunity to gaze upon a transformation within and clearly see how fate and destiny draws one to them.

I began this quest to inform men that we too are subject to the disease called breast cancer. Along the way, a window opened, allowing in reflection, the acknowledgement of fears and challenges, different experiences, and the capacity to fully embrace the healing. As I delved deeper and exposed various facets of my travels, I received additional gifts. I was able to witness again the birth of my empowerment in directing a personal path in my passage to heal.

Every doctor, nurse, healer, colleague, friend, family member, partner, and acquaintance was a teacher. In this restorative sojourn, I explored places deep inside and harnessed the might to heal within.

Throughout this crossing, gratitude was only magnified. Where once I may have taken people, situations, or emotions for granted, now I value their meaning and gift in my healing destiny.

Arising from the second diagnosis in 2010 was an intuitive awakening in receiving the positive energy from others. I had entered a new realm, where energy from thoughts, actions, intentions, prayers, and presence of other living beings was consciously felt, embraced, and embedded. They became an integral healer in my journey. As Deepak Chopra writes, "The gifts of caring, attention, affection, appreciation, and love are some of the most precious gifts you can give."

The gratitude felt for these bestowals became an intoxicating cure on its own. I discovered that the more gratitude I held and extended to others, the more of this healing wonder was returned.

In reflection on the voyage shared in this book, the most precious, most authentic gift was connecting with my inner being. It is where I trusted and followed the guidance emanating from my heart, my inner voice, and my soul.

The opening of my heart created a welcoming space for spirituality. My spirituality granted peace, direction, and trust.

For some, a healing path may embody the tenets of a deep religious faith or the discovery and embracing of one's spirituality. It may be a passage firmly planted within a traditional medicinal route, a holistic direction, or a combination of both. A true healing will arise when empowering the heart, not fear. For any route traveled when guided by the heart and one's soul is a true path, your true journey to heal.

Healing Within

The ultimate discovery in my journey with breast cancer was what was hidden within. Michael Meade put it best when he wrote, "When the heart within the heart opens, the issue becomes not simply *who* I am or appear to be, but *what* is hidden within me."

My expedition to heal within initiated a self-evolution. This intense pilgrimage has enriched my heart, my soul, and my life in countless manners. Hidden in the depths of my being, strength, trust, love, courage, and peace gained their freedom. Once freed, these closeted gifts dispensed a faith in new ways of healing.

The familiar Quaker phrase, *the way will open*, became a reality once I had complete trust in my heart and soul in guiding me to where I needed to be.

In my journey with cancer, the hidden gifts within emerged when I awakened to their crusade and healing power by surrendering to the universe and trusting they knew the way.

May you discover what is hidden within, and may your journey be filled with peace.

In the Present

*The true wisdom of one's life lies deep within and tends
to appear when the truth of the situation is faced.*

Michael Meade

On a cold, dreary January day in 2007, a terrified man exited his doctor's office a new member in the growing ranks of breast cancer's family. With that diagnosis, a journey unfolded.

Over time, as the passage unveiled new paths, fear—which had been a leading force in my life—was displaced and carefully given a new position in this pilgrimage. It is still present, but now a controlled necessity, an ally in a sense, assisting to keep things in balance. It has assumed the role of a teacher, for when fear's tentacles are frantically seeking to take hold, I simply recognize its existence. Sitting quietly, focusing on my breath, I ask, "What do I need to know or learn?"

In time, the answer reveals itself, uncovering the source of the fear. I acknowledge its presence, its gift of a lesson, and allow it to dissipate into the vastness of space. Then, utilizing the tools acquired, I compassionately and without judgment dismember the problem or situation.

During these past seven years, I attained an inner peace, fostering an understanding, an acceptance that cancer will be an integral part of my life. But, like fear, it has been relegated to the back seat in the drive to heal. Its effects, while touching many facets of daily living, are minimized, as I am no longer in denial or terrified of its existence, but grateful for its many gifts.

An emotional deepness in listening to my heart and soul has awakened a stronger, more intuitive being.

In the period of my healing education, I've obtained a meaningful grasp of what is important and what is not. I am conscious of the significance in removing myself or creating a distance from toxic environments and individuals whose presence hinders my healing. I have learned to empower my inner self, the voice of guidance, my soul, my spirit.

I continue to incorporate meditation, promoting quiet moments of listening, learning, and peace.

This remarkable journey revealed a hidden wisdom. One obscured from sight but silently, patiently waiting until a call for action, an invitation was extended by the surrendering of my entire being to the universe.

This act of self-love awarded the inner sagacity its freedom. Its liberation nurtured a self-acceptance and a confirmation of trust in the new path I was venturing down.

In the present, I strive to live in the moment, to possess my spirit, embrace its importance, and not let it disappear into the depths of my being. To be in the moment allows me to live, love, and enjoy now, for that is truly all I have.

I relish the simple pleasures like the sight of our dog, Polar, carrying his treasured ball gripped tightly in his jaws as we explore the back fields. I observe his sister, Macy, as she roams the open space, taking in its various scents, and I swear she is smiling. I cherish my loving connections to friends and family, my life with Tim, and the acceptance of being me.

Each day, I learned to listen to the gentle whispers of my heart, the song of healing from my soul, and the essence of my being, for they are who I am.

My quest unveiled the knowledge of my cancer's relationship to the long-held belief that I was not good enough.

With this judgment secured in every fiber of my being, I overcompensated by putting others' needs before mine; I overworked and overstressed my emotional inner spirit. It was easy and quite natural to blame others and especially myself, thereby becoming the victim. In this mode, I was blind to the power of forgiveness.

At the core of healing, forgiveness allows the letting go of those who may have betrayed, deserted, or hurt me at one time, but it also provided the gift of self-forgiveness.

When I lacked self-compassion or the ability to extend empathy, the rise of an inner anger and resentment furnished the perfect lodging for disease. The illness was at home, and fear kept it supplied, content, and granted it freedom to roam and conquer.

With my blessing, fear amassed the power to take prisoner the strength I needed. It confined within its parameters my thoughts, choices, and actions, disabling any capability to live fully in the present. Fear was a resident for so long, I did not possess the might or proficiency to battle its forces. I had succumbed to its poisonous control.

The universe, this higher power of love, watched and waited until it no longer would allow the overtaking of my soul. In its infinite wisdom, the universe gifted an act of love, awakening my inner being.

In this journey, I have procured the necessary tools to ease out of each noxious element that pollutes and sidetracks my healing.

I am now able to make essential changes when these circumstances arise. Times when I may fall under the spell of fear, anger, or resentment, when I may resort to old fear-enabling behaviors, or when I may stumble into their trap, are when the tools are put to use. I stop and catch myself in its midst by returning to the present moment, focusing on my breath, and releasing the unwanted visitor.

For a majority of my life, the feeling of not being good enough, not deserving self-love, and the feeling that I would never get it all right controlled many facets of a potential to truly live. I expected and strived to attain perfection in all aspects of myself, believing this was the only way to banish these thoughts and convictions.

What I have learned from my passage with cancer is that perfection is not a reality; it is not life; it is not living. With open arms, I now welcome the actuality of these draining actions. It was a rude but realistic awakening and a self-loving gesture.

A wonderful, teachable moment happened when I read a statement in Pema Chodron's book, *Start Where You Are: A Guide for Compassionate Living*, where in attending one of her first Buddhist teachings, the teacher stated, "I don't know why you came here, but I want to tell you right now, that the basis of this whole teaching is that you're never going to get everything together."

As I read those words, they opened a part deep within and made me take notice. Too often in my pre-cancer and early-cancer life, I would continuously throw myself down emotionally, because I could not get every facet of my life right. No sooner had I overcome some obstacle and rejoiced in the accomplishment than another hurdle that had been waiting on the sidelines suddenly appeared and took center stage and control. There always seemed to be something.

An invaluable lesson was the realization that I will never get it all right or all together. That is not living. It is not living fully and in the present.

I now embrace the knowledge and tools in not giving power to what is not all together in my life and trust an important teaching will emerge from its presence.

According to many enlightened individuals, we are entering a shift to a new era, a more informed time. We are exiting a shadowy realm to one engulfed with light. In this period, I take notice of those I am with. They are my traveling companions as I enter this new realm of time and energy.

These gentle beings gift the essence of their soul as my guide. They are my flashlight, a bright torch when darkness envelops my path. They have taken on the attributes of a trusted walking stick, the rock formations upon which I can lay my hand for safety and security as I follow this quest to discover my destiny. These like-minded spirits are present to nurture, to feed, and comfort, so that I may proceed with this healing passage.

I welcome, embrace, and cherish each soul, for they are present in my sojourn as I am in theirs.

My journey to heal is ongoing, and I am grateful to the many dedicated and loving companions who grace this path I travel. My physicians, healers, family, friends, and Tim are all partners and teachers in my crusade to heal.

Along the way, I extended my circle of healers with the inclusion of Shiatsu massage. Elin, my Shiatsu therapist, provides this bodywork, which supports and strengthens the natural ability of my body to heal and balance itself. This practice complements the therapies I receive from Maud, John, Zaidee, and Bridgette.

In our sessions, Elin uses touch, comfortable pressure, and stretches to adjust my body's physical structure and balance its energy flow. Like my other energy-based therapies, Shiatsu works on my whole being—the physical body in concert with the psychological, emotional, and spiritual being.

For a few months, while composing this book, I was traveling to Rupert, Vermont, to spend time with Rupa Cousins, a Rubenfeld synergist. Our sessions involved talk-touch-imagination modalities, assisting me to delve even deeper to connect and explore new healing avenues.

The diagnosis of breast cancer gifted this remarkable journey to heal within, and in the process, I discovered my true self and the strength to face fear, to take risks, and to follow a dream.

Thank you for being part of this healing journey.

Helpful Connections

Capital Region Action Against Breast Cancer (CRAAB)
125 Wolf Road—Suite 124
Albany, New York 12205
Phone: (518) 435-1055
craab@nycap.rr.com

Yoga
Align Again Yoga—Zaidee Bliss
70 Main Street
Greenwich, New York 12834
www.alignagainyoga.com

Reiki
Integrated Energy Practice, Equine Reiki, Queen B Balms—
Maud Maynard—Reiki Master
maudmaynardreiki@wordpress.com

Maud recommends the following website:
www.reikimedicine.com

Acupuncture
Ageless Acupuncture—Bridgette Kinder, L.Ac.
www.agelessinsaratoga.com

Energy Medicine
Winged Spirit Healing—An Integrative Approach to Energy Medicine
John Hearst, MD
jhnhrst@gmail.com

John recommends the following sites for additional information:
www.rosalynbruyere.org
www.altarofcreation.com

Alternative Health Care of Western MA, Inc.
Gary S. Lasneski, DC, MS
59 Interstate Drive
West Springfield, Massachusetts 01089
Phone: (413) 455-2168
www.alternativehealthcarewesternmass.com

Psychic and Medium
Psychic and Medium Consultations: For Spiritual Enlightenment and Peace
Tracy Elizabeth Fluty
Tracy@tracyfluty.com
www.tracyfluty.com

Holistic Health Counselor
Maddie Sobel
www.maddiesobelwellness.com

Shamanic Healing

Carol recommended the following sources of information on shamanic healing:

Awakening to the Spirit World: The Shamanic Path of Direct Revelation, by S. Ingerman and H. Wesselman

Spirited Medicine: Shamanism in Contemporary Healthcare. Available from the Society for Shamanic Practioners
www.shamansociety.org

Soul Retrieval: Mending the Fragmented Self, by S. Ingerman

www.shamanicteachers.com
www.sandraingerman.com

Rubenfeld Synergy Therapy
www.rubenfeldsynergy.com
www.rupacousins.com

Shiatsu
Elements of Bodywork
Elin Cary
www.elementsofbodyworkmt.com

Acknowledgments

It is here that I wish to express my immense gratitude to all who have been and are treasured spirits in my journey to heal within.

To my wonderful team of physicians, to whom I am forever grateful: Dr. Robert M. Kelleher—I am fortunate to have your presence in my journey; Dr. Janet Gargiulo (Dr. G.)—you are a gift I cherish; Dr. Muhammad Hena—thank you for your skill and expertise; Dr. Charlene Ives—I thank you for your support, respect, and guidance; Dr. Joseph D. Choma—a wonderful connection was made the minute you entered the room. I thank you; Dr. Anthony Donaldson—I am grateful that you are part of this team; physician assistant Rachele Gates—you are a joy!; Dr. Noonan, Dr. Rockmore—thank you for being part of this journey; Dr. Resta—thank you for not only your expertise but for being my teacher.

To the healers this universe carefully, patiently, and lovingly guided my path to cross: Zaidee Bliss—you are instrumental with connections to other healers; Maud Maynard—you are not only my Reiki healer, but a friend and treasured gift; Bridgette Kinder—I always look forward to our healing sessions; John Hearst—your gentle presence in my journey and the connections you inspired are cherished; Dr. Lasneski—you gave me a new insight; Cory McCarthy— you tenderly guided me to a new light; Tracy Fluty—your gift is warmth and a relationship to not only those who have passed, but to myself; Mary Muncil—your spiritual insight allowed me to grow and follow a dream; Carol Tunney—I am forever grateful that our life paths crossed before you left this physical world—thank you; Elin Cary—your gift is your spirit; Rupa Cousins—you guided my inner eyes and self to see more clearly; Diane Lange—I am eternally grateful for your tattoo artistry, which has helped me feel whole; Maddie Sobel—thank you for sharing your delicious and nutritious knowledge.

I would also like to thank the Capital Region Action Against Breast Cancer for the work, guidance, and support given to so many.

To those who took the time to read my manuscript in progress and provide wonderful insights, encouragement, and love: Peter Franceschetti, CeCe Pittman, Maud Maynard, Eileen Bruni, John Hearst, Dan McIntyre, Ronnie Delancey-Smith, Dan Winokur and Jenna Lord, Helen Kovarik, Felicitas Anderson, and Tim Watkins. Thank you!

To my friends whose love, support, and energy grace me each day in this journey of life: Peter Franceschetti and Chuck Krulis, CeCe Pittman, Jane Ebaugh, Mike Kuzniar, Christine Gaudet and Diane Yorke, Ronnie Delancey-Smith—you are family that I treasure; Maud Maynard—you are light; Alison Preville—my radiation soul mate; Sue Nadeau—thank you for being there; Tish Walker—you will always be a part of my life; Scott Smith and Ed Hale—the physical distance between us has not diminished what you both mean to me; Eleanor Walters—you are a treasured friend; Eileen Bruni—our connection, our talks are uplifting; John Williams—my Texas brother; Karen Costello—you are cherished; Jane Elvin—I am forever grateful to you for sharing your journey with me; Whit Merrill—your words changed my course; Gerard Golden and Tony Lofrumento—your friendship is priceless; Dixon Rice—you were there at the beginning and I thank you; Debbie Strugar—you make me laugh.

To Lee Shapiro and Patrick Gill, John Clark, Steven Cowart, Rob Haren and David Bassani, Rob Bauer and Peter Subers, David Armbrewster, Jeff Bowers and Milton Ilario, Mike Diaz, Ed Hutchins and Steve Warren—Washington County had graciously gifted you to my life. Thank you.

To the staff, students, and parents at Veeder Elementary School—thank you so much.

To Connie and Kate at my home away from home—Battenkill Books in Cambridge, New York—thank you!

To Jenna Woginrich—you have been an inspiration in this journey. Listening to you share your memoir, *Barnheart*, at Battenkill Books was when the dream of writing began.

To Chrissy and Steve Froehlich—Tim and I can't say thank you enough for your gift of Polar and Macy.

To Dr. Menard and the wonderful individuals at Borador Animal Hospital in Salem, New York—thank you for taking care of Polar and Macy.

To my yoga soul mates at *Seventy Main* in Greenwich, New York—namaste'.

To Felicitas Anderson—you have touched my soul.

To the many valiant women who have journeyed with this disease—I am forever in your debt.

To my niece Kaitlyn Tolman—I thank you from my heart for your insight, knowledge, love, and for being you.

To Louise Jones—thank you for respecting my voice while editing this journey.

To Nikki Osbun, Stephanie Cornthwaite, Andrew Carter, and Adriane Pontecorvo at Balboa Press––thank you.

To Dana Pierson at Balboa Press––thank you for your final editing skills.

To my wonderful family: my mom—Helen Kovarik, my brother Chuck Kovarik, my sister-in-law Carolyn, my nephew Brian and his fiancée—Cara, my nephews Danny, and James, and my niece Amie; my sister—Janet Mahoney, my brother-in-law Jack, my nephew Ryan and wife Danielle and my charming grand niece Reagan, my niece Kaitlyn Tolman and husband Joseph, my nephew Kyle and wife Anine and new addition Kaleigh Jade—Thank you for being an important part of my life and journey. Your love, caring, energy, and support are received each day. I love you all.

To the Watkins family—thank you for your love and welcoming spirit.

To Tim Watkins—I am grateful for your wonderful and loving presence in my life.

Bibliography

Page xi, *"Let your actions and words come forth slowly …"* Dan Millman. *The Laws of Spirit: A Tale of Transformation: Powerful Truths for Making Life Work.* 1995 by Dan Millman. (HJ Kramer Book-Tiburon, CA in joint venture with New World Library-Novato, CA). Page 16.

Page 1, *"The real journey of life aims …"* Michael Meade. *Fate and Destiny: The Two Agreements of the Soul.* Second Edition 2012 by Michael J. Meade. Original copyright 2010 by Michael J. Meade. (Greenfire Press: An Imprint of Mosaic Multicultural Foundation-Seattle, WA). Page 187.

Page 4, *"Even the thought of giving …"* Deepak Chopra. *The Seven Spiritual Laws of Success: A Practical Guide to the Fulfillment of Your Dreams.* 1994 by Deepak Chopra. Based on the book *Creating Affluence: Wealth Consciousness in the Field of all Possibilities.* 1993 by Deepak Chopra. (Co-published by Amber-Allen Publishing, San Rafael, CA and New World Library-Novato, CA). Page 31.

Page 11, *"Fear is a natural reaction to moving closer …"* Pema Chodron. *When Things Fall Apart: Heart Advice for Difficult Times.* 1997 by Pema Chodron. (Shambhala Publications, Inc., Boston, MA). Page 2.

Page 13, *"Balance begins with the breath."* Dan Millman. *The Laws of Spirit: A Tale of Transformation: Powerful Truths for Making Life Work.* 1995 by Dan Millman. (HJ Kramer Book, Tiburon, CA in joint venture with New World Library, Novato, CA). Page 15.

Page 14, *"Our fate will bring us to a crossroads …"* Michael Meade. *Fate and Destiny: The Two Agreements of the Soul.* Second Edition 2012 by Michael J. Meade. Original copyright 2010 by Michael J. Meade. (Greenfire Press: An Imprint of Mosaic Multicultural Foundation, Seattle, WA). Page 240.

Page 19, *" …study the prison you have built around yourself by inadvertence."* Sri Nisargadatta Maharaj. *I Am That: Talks with Sri*

Nisargadatta Maharaj. 1973 by Nisargadatta Maharaj. Originally published by Chetana Pvt. Ltd.-Bombay 1973. (Published by arrangement with Chetana, in the USA and Canada, Acorn Press, Durham, NC). Page 5.

Page 22, "*A certain kind of courage ...*" Michael Meade. *Fate and Destiny: The Two Agreements of the Soul*. Second Edition 2012 by Michael J. Meade. Original copyright 2010 by Michael J. Meade. (Greenfire Press: An Imprint of Mosaic Multicultural Foundation, Seattle, WA). Page 154.

Page 24, "*Faith means living with uncertainty.*" Dan Millman. *The Laws of Spirit: A Tale of Transformation: Powerful Truths for Making Life Work*. 1995 by Dan Millman. (HJ Kramer Book-Tiburon, CA, in joint venture with New World Library, Novato, CA). Page 55.

Page 31, "*Without trust there is no peace.*" Sri Nisargadatta Maharaj. *I Am That: Talks with Sri Nisargadatta Maharaj*. 1973 Nisargadatta Maharaj. Originally published by Chetana Pvt. Ltd., Bombay, 1973. (Published by arrangement with Chetana, in the USA and Canada, Acorn Press, Durham, NC). Page 149.

Page 32, CD—*Prepare Your Body for Surgery and Recovery*. Sue Van Hook. Recorded by Alan Bartenhagen. Northern Roads Productions. *Peaceful Music for Anything* by Carl Landa.

Page 33, "*Surrender involves getting out of our own way ...*" Dan Millman. *The Laws of Spirit: A Tale of Transformation: Powerful Truths for Making Life Work*. 1995 by Dan Millman. (HJ Kramer Book, Tiburon, CA, in joint venture with New World Library, Novato, CA). Page 89.

Page 42, "*Ultimately each person holds the key to the story ...*" Michael Meade. *Fate and Destiny: The Two Agreements of the Soul*. Second Edition 2012 by Michael J. Meade. Original copyright 2010 by Michael J. Meade. (Greenfire Press: An Imprint of Mosaic Multicultural Foundation, Seattle, WA). Page 122.

Page 43, "*We must consult our deep hearts ...*" Meredith L. Young-Sowers. *Spirit Heals: Awakening a Woman's Inner Knowing for Self Healing.* 2007 by Meredith L. Young-Sowers. (New World Library, Novato, CA). Page 21.

Page 48, "*...listen to the intuitive wisdom ...*" Dan Millman. *The Laws of Spirit: A Tale of Transformation: Powerful Truths for Making Life Work.* 1995 by Dan Millman. (HJ Kramer Book, Tiburon, CA, in joint venture with New World Library, Novato, CA). Page 53.

Page 51, "*Healing requires taking ...*" Caroline Myss. *Anatomy of the Spirit: The Seven Stages of Power and Healing.* 1996 by Caroline Myss. (Three Rivers Press, New York). Page 57.

Page 56, "*...the wounds and the poisons we encounter ...*" Michael Meade. *Fate and Destiny: The Two Agreements of the Soul.* Second Edition 2012 by Michael J. Meade. Original copyright 2010 by Michael J. Meade. (Greenfire Press: An Imprint of Mosaic Multicultural Foundation, Seattle, WA). Page 314.

Page 59, "*...nothing is impossible when we follow ...*" Gerald G. Jampolsky, MD. *Love is Letting Go of Fear.* Third Edition. Copyright 1979, 2004, 2011 by Gerald G. Jampolsky, MD. (Celestial Arts: An Imprint of the Crown Publishing Group, a division of Random House, Inc., New York). Page 86.

Page 71, "*If in our daily lives we can smile ...*" Thich Nhat Hanh. *Peace is Every Step: The Path of Mindfulness in Everyday Life.* 1991 by Thich Nhat Hanh. (Bantam Books, New York). Page 6.

Page 72, *Insight Meditation: Workbook.* Sharon Salzberg and Joseph Goldstein. 2001 by Sharon Salzberg and Joseph Goldstein. (Sounds True, Boulder, CO).

Page 76, "*May I be filled with loving-kindness ...*" Reprinted in *Spirit Heals: Awakening a Woman's Inner Knowing for Self Healing.* 2007 by Meredith L. Young-Sowers. (New World Library, Novato, CA). Page 43. Used with permission from *A Path With Heart: A Guide Through the Perils and Promises of Spiritual Life.* 1993 Jack Kornfield. (Bantam Books, New York).

Page 77, *"The spiritual journey involves..."* Pema Chodron. *When Things Fall Apart: Heart Advice for Difficult Times.* 1997 by Pema Chodron. (Shambhala Publications, Boston, MA). Page 15.

Page 78, *"Resentment long held..."* Louise L. Hay. *You Can Heal Your Life.* 1984, 1987, 2004 by Louise L. Hay. (Hay House, Inc., Carlsbad, CA). Pages 6–7.

Page 78, *"I have found that forgiving..."* Louise L. Hay. *You Can Heal Your Life.* 1984, 1987, 2004 by Louise L. Hay. (Hay House, Inc., Carlsbad, CA). Page 7.

Page 79, *"I forgive you for not being..."* Louise L. Hay. *You Can Heal Your Life.* 1984, 1987, 2004 by Louise L. Hay. (Hay House, Inc., Carlsbad, CA). Page 8.

Page 85, *"...yet our healing journey is all about change."* Meredith L. Young-Sowers. *Spirit Heals: Awakening a Woman's Inner Knowing for Self Healing.* 2007 by Meredith L. Young-Sowers. (New World Library, Novato, CA). Page 53.

Page 94, *"The well is within us..."* Thich Nhat Hanh. *Peace is Every Step: The Path of Mindfulness in Everyday Life.* 1991 by Thich Nhat Hanh. (Bantam Books, New York). Page 41.

Page 97, *"Usually we're so caught up in ourselves..."* Pema Chodron. *Start Where You Are: A Guide to Compassionate Living.* 1994 by Pema Chodron. (2004 Shambhala Publications, Boston, MA). Page 111.

Page 102, *"We are our most whole..."* Michael Meade. *Fate and Destiny: The Two Agreements of the Soul.* Second Edition 2012 by Michael J. Meade. Original copyright 2010 by Michael J. Meade. (Greenfire Press: An Imprint of Mosaic Multicultural Foundation, Seattle, WA). Page 168.

Page 106, "*Create a new version of who you would become* …" Dan Millman. *The Laws of Spirit: A Tale of Transformation: Powerful Truths for Making Life Work*. 1995 by Dan Millman. (HJ Kramer Book, Tiburon, CA, in joint venture with New World Library, Novato, CA). Page 64.

Page 109, "*Notice the blue sky* …" Thich Nhat Hanh. *Peace is Every Step: The Path of Mindfulness in Everyday Life*. 1991 by Thich Nhat Hanh. (Bantam Books, New York). Page XIV.

Page 110, "*Every time we get back in touch* …" Thich Nhat Hanh. *Peace is Every Step: The Path of Mindfulness in Everyday Life*. 1991 by Thich Nhat Hanh. (Bantam Books, New York). Page 19.

Page 115, "*Now is the time* …" Meredith L. Young-Sowers. *Spirit Heals: Awakening a Woman's Inner Knowing for Self Healing*. 2007 by Meredith L. Young-Sowers. (New World Library, Novato, CA). Page 16.

Page 118, "*Many drown in the commotion of life* …" Michael Meade. *Fate and Destiny: The Two Agreements of the Soul*. Second Edition 2012 by Michael J. Meade. Original copyright 2010 by Michael J. Meade. (Greenfire Press: An Imprint of Mosaic Multicultural Foundation, Seattle, WA). Page 149.

Page 119, "*Being fully awake means* …" Michael Meade. *Fate and Destiny: The Two Agreements of the Soul*. Second Edition 2012 by Michael J. Meade. Original copyright 2010 by Michael J. Meade. (Greenfire Press: An Imprint of Mosaic Multicultural Foundation, Seattle, WA). Page 150.

Page 120, "*The gifts of caring, attention* …" Deepak Chopra. *The Seven Spiritual Laws of Success: A Practical Guide to the Fulfillment of Your Dreams*. 1994 by Deepak Chopra. Based on the book *Creating Affluence: Wealth Consciousness in the Field of all Possibilities*. 1993 by Deepak Chopra. (Co-published by Amber-Allen Publishing, San Rafael, CA and New World Library, Novato, CA). Page 32.

Page 121, "*When the heart within ...*" Michael Meade. *Fate and Destiny: The Two Agreements of the Soul.* Second Edition 2012 by Michael J. Meade. Original copyright 2010 by Michael J. Meade. (Greenfire Press: An Imprint of Mosaic Multicultural Foundation, Seattle, WA). Page 200.

Page 122, "*The true wisdom of one's life ...*" Michael Meade. *Fate and Destiny: The Two Agreements of the Soul.* Second Edition 2012 by Michael J. Meade. Original copyright 2010 by Michael J. Meade. (Greenfire Press: An Imprint of Mosaic Multicultural Foundation, Seattle, WA). Page 308.

Page 124, "*I don't know why ...*" Pema Chodron. *Start Where You Are: A Guide to Compassionate Living.* 1994 by Pema Chodron. (Shambhala Publications, Inc., Boston, MA). Page 138.

About the Author

Michael was born in 1956 in New York City. He spent his childhood and early adult life in Pearl River, New York.

Upon graduating high school, Michael attended Rockland Community College and Penn State University, where he attained a degree in elementary education.

His teaching career spanned thirty-four years, with experiences in New Hampshire, Virginia, and upstate New York. While living and teaching in Virginia, Michael completed a master's program in educational administration from the College of William and Mary.

In 2007, a new journey began with the diagnosis of breast cancer, but it was with the second occurrence of this disease in 2010, when a deeper determination to heal within was born.

It was within this journey to heal that the dream to write about his passage unfolded.

Michael currently lives in Greenwich, New York, with his partner, Tim Watkins, and their dogs, Polar and Macy.

You can contact Michael at:
mwk.healing@gmailcom
or
www.facebook.com/mwk.healing

CPSIA information can be obtained at www.ICGtesting.com
Printed in the USA
BVOW07s2125240614

357258BV00001B/1/P